RELATIONSHIPS:
ARE THEY WORTH THE TIME AND EFFORT?

Also featuring:

DATING: DOES ANYONE DO IT ANYMORE?

By Randy Wallace

These are short topics my female reader said they would like for me to address. These are some of the areas they see where a woman needs help when it comes to relationships.

www.writersblockpublishing.net

Written by Randy Wallace at rwrelationship@yahoo.com.
Facebook: Randy Wallace of Dallas, Texas.

FORWARD

Relationships: It seems like more people are in them and a lot more people are trying to get into them. I want you to take a minute to think about the relationship you are in now, your past relationships, and the ones that you may be trying to start for the future. Ask yourself: given all that you have learned about your past relationships, is it worth trying to start a new one? Are they worth the time and effort that goes into them? Did you get as much out of the relationship as you put into it? Was the person you were with as committed to making the relationship work as you were? Did you put months or years into a new relationship only to have it end because the person you were with was not as committed to the relationship as you were? Did the relationship end because of new problems, old problems, or repeated problems? Did you truly know the person you were with while you were in that relationship or did you just think you knew them? These are some of the questions I think people need to ask themselves about a new, old, or present relationship.

Relationships are good when they are good, but what happens to a relationship when there is a problem or problems? Ask yourself, how did you and the person you were with in your last relationship deal with problems when they came up? Were you able to talk and communicate about concerns and issues in the relationship? Was there a suitable way for both of you to solve problems when they came up? Or did you just keep having the same problems with no solutions? Did both of you think the relationship was worth saving? Did the relationship have a future? Do you think the relationship could have led to marriage? Did the relationship have time to grow and reach its full potential? With all of these things in mind, are relationships worth the time and effort you put into them? Is what you get out of them worth it?

I'm not saying all relationships are bad or will end badly. What I am saying is all relationships takes work and commitment by both people involved. If this is not in place in your relationship, then one person will end up working harder to make it work than the other. When the relationship ends, you walk away mentally and physically exhausted and confused, asking yourself: Was this relationship worth all of that time and effort?

WHAT LOVE WILL MAKE YOU DO

Love will cause you make a permanent decision about a person based on the temporary things they do for you. You will make a decision to be with a person based on what you want from them and how you see them. You love the way they look, you love the way they make love to you, you love the money they give you, and all the things they do for you. You love all of these things so much you allow them to physically abuse you, disrespect you, cheat on you, break your heart, and lie to you. You surrender yourself, your mind, your body, and your sense of purpose to a person all because you love them and the things they do for you in the name of love. Love will make you remain committed to a person, knowing all the time they are not committed to you. Some people pay the ultimate price for love only to find out the price they paid was not worth the love they received. Here is a list of things love will make you do:

1) Love will make you give up your family, friends, and child or children.
2) Love will make you give up your morals, values, and cause you have low self-esteem.
3) Love will make you spend hours trying to catch a person cheating, but do nothing when you catch them out of the love you have for them.
4) Love will make you do things you thought you would never do.
5) Love will make you do the wrong thing when you know the right thing to do.
6) Love will break your heart.
7) Love will allow you to accept hurt and pain from that broken heart.
8) Love will allow you to accept the fact that you love a person that doesn't love you.
9) Love will make you stay committed to a person that is not committed to you.

10) The love you have for another person will make you stop loving yourself.

These are just ten things people will do for love, but there are lots more. My questions to you are: What would you do for love? What have you done for love?

ACCEPT THE REALITY OF YOUR RELATIONSHIP

My readers ask me if I am a relationship expert. I tell them, "No!" But I do deal with reality of the relationships. I tell my readers they must deal with the reality of their marriage or relationship and make a decision based on that to stay or leave. You must accept the choices you made in your relationship, good or bad. Learn from them and use what you learned to make better choices going forward. The reality is people enter into relationships knowing the person they are with may not be the right person for them. If a person is not an asset to you, then they will be a liability to you. Let me ask you this: remember when you were back in school? Your teacher would trust you to grade your own homework paper, all she asked is that you were honest about doing it. I am going to ask you to do the same thing with you relationship. Be honest and truthful with yourself. Give your relationship the grade it deserves.

A. Great, could not be better.
B. Good, but needs work.
C. I have done all I can do and nothing is working.
D. I don't see anything getting better.
E. I know the relationship is over. It is time for me to move on with my life.

What grade did you give your relationship?

- If a person is cheating on you while you are dating them, what makes you think they will stop just because you are in a relationship with them?
- If you are in a relationship with a person that cheats on you, what makes you think they will stop just because you marry them?
- If you marry a person that cheated in the relationship, what makes you think they will stop just because you are now married to them?

The reality is people make a choice to be with a person for whatever the reason. They think the person will change or stop doing what they were doing when they met them. The majority of the time, a person knows what kind of person they chose to be with. Sometimes they don't, but when a person shows you who they are and it is not what you expected, why do you stay? If they had misled you, then what makes you think they will stop? If you stay with them, then the reality is what happens next is on you. If you choose to stay with that person knowing who they are, you have no one to blame but yourself for the way they treat you. You must accept the reality of your choice and not blame them for being who they are when you met them. The reality of life is not all people are good people, not all people will be who or what they say they are, not all people will have your best interest at heart, and not all people can be trusted. If you are in a relationship and the person you are with is one or all of these things and you stay with them, the reality is you fooling yourself. They are not fooling you.

CHEATING IN THE RELATIONSHIP

Unfortunately, this is the most common relationship people find themselves in through no fault of their own. Most people enter into relationship thinking the person they are with will be as loyal and faithful to them as they are to the person they are with. Some people enter into a relationship with a person knowing they are a cheater or they have cheated in a past relationship. Let me say this: there is no good reason for a person to cheat, only bad excuses. If you are in a relationship, then you love or have strong feelings for the person you are with.

Love: there are many definitions for love and people show it in many different ways. Think about the people you love: your mother father, siblings, child or children, family friends, or pets. No matter who you love, you will never do anything to hurt them. So if you are in a relationship with a person and they say they love you but cheat on you, disrespect you, physically and verbally abuse you, what kind of love is that? Is there a new kind of love that I don't know about? Is this the kind of love the only two people in a relationship can share? Is this the kind of love people raised their child or children to show other people? Is this the only kind of love some people will accept? In my book, Why Do Men Cheat, and Cheating: Men, How to Do it Right - A Guide for the Cheating Man, I talked about these things and this is what I said.

CHEATING

Cheating is a premeditated act. It takes timing, preparation, planning, and money. People are still willing to put all that time and effort to do it. If a person cheats knowing if they get caught they can lose their marriage or relationship, family, home, the love of the person they are with, and they still make the decision to cheat, what does that say about them? If you stay with a person that is willing to put all that time and effort into cheating knowing they have all of those things to lose if caught cheating and still do it, what does that say about you? People do not need a reason to cheat, but they do need someone to blame their cheating on or some excuse when they get caught. Usually, it is not their fault. It is the fault of the person they are cheating on. People know that when they get caught cheating, it will hurt the person they are with, but they are willing to risk all of that for a few minutes of pleasure. They know that it will cause the person they are with a lifetime of pain and hurt, but they choose to cheat anyway. And they say they love you. We said earlier that love is not supposed to hurt. Then why are you hurting?

CHEATING: WHAT YOUR SPOUSE, MAN OR WOMAN CAN SHARE WITH YOU

We all know in a marriage or relationship, the two people in it share just about everything. In a marriage or relationship, if your spouse, man, or woman is cheating, then they can share with you some of the things they receive from cheating. Here are a few things they can share:

1) HIV or AIDS
2) Syphilis
3) Gonorrhea
4) Chlamydia
5) Herpes
6) Genital Warts

7) An unwanted pregnancy where the mother doesn't know who the father of her child is
8) A pregnancy where the man denies he is the father of a child
9) Broken heart
10) The trust you had in them

These are just a few things your spouse, man or woman can get from cheating, then come home and share it with you. Maybe they have already shared STD with you and you stayed. You stay because you are in denial and you don't love yourself enough to save your life. So, if your spouse, man or woman gives you a STD, you need to say a prayer and thank God that is all that you have.

WHY DOES MY MAN'S BREATH SMELL LIKE FISH?

Ladies, I hear you say this all the time. "My man's breath smelled like fish when he came from the club or when he says he's been hanging out with his boys." But he doesn't have a fishing pole or any fish when he comes home and all the seafood restaurants and fish markets are closed. Ask yourself, ladies, what other thing do you know that smells like fish? You already know the answer. The same thing he is doing to you sexually, he is doing with the woman he is cheating with. You let him put the same tongue in your mouth that he used to give her oral pleasure. You ask him why his breath smells like fish. This is because he has been eating something that smells like fish. You know this, but you are in denial. The thing he does to you sexually that gives you pleasure, he is doing the same thing to her. You still accept him and that fish smell that is coming from his breath. You let his lips kiss yours and kiss your children, knowing where they have been and what he has been doing. You convince yourself that if you wait a few days, everything will be alright. He will eventually brush his teeth or use some mouthwash to remove the smell. Then you forgive him until the next weekend he comes home with breath smelling like fish. You accept this because you love him more than you love yourself. One day, he will share something with you that he got from cheating with her.

Ladies, my mother had a saying that went like this. A woman is just like a tea bag you never know how strong it is till you put it in hot water and drink it. You will never know how strong you are until you believe how strong you can be. You can't blame a person for the way they treat you, but you can blame yourself for allowing them to treat you that way.

TRUST IN A RELATIONSHIP

We talked about cheating in a relationship. Now I want to talk about trust.

Do you trust the person in your relationship?   Yes or No.
Does the person you are with trust you?   Yes or No.

If the answer is yes to both questions, that's great. That means that your relationship is on the right track. If the answer is no, then my question to you is why you are still with them? Why are they still with you? If you two don't have the most common thing in your relationship, trust, to make it work, then why are you two still together?

Did the person you are with do something to you that caused you to lose your trust in them?   Yes or No.

Did you do something to them to cause them to lose trust in you?   Yes or No.

If the answer to both questions is yes, why are you with them? You will trust your life to a person but you will not trust them with your cell phone. You will give over your heart freely to a person, but you will not give them your cell phone password. You will do just about anything to keep the person you are with from seeing it, or they will do anything to keep you from seeing theirs. You will trust a person with your body, but you will not trust them with your Facebook password. Do you have a GPS device on their cell phone or car? You have to do all of these things just to stay with the person you are married to or in a relationship. There is nothing wrong with them; there is something wrong with you.

Let's review the things you do to trust your spouse, man, or woman with and the things you don't trust them with. These are some things married couples and couples in a relationship told me about the person they are with.

THINGS YOU TRUST THEM WITH

1) Your heart
2) Your body
3) Your life

THINGS YOU DON'T TRUST THEM WITH

1) Your cell phone
2) Your cell phone password
3) Your Facebook password
4) Your purse or wallet
5) Your ATM card and number, credit card, or your money
6) What they say
7) What they say they've been doing
8) Where they say they've been
9) Who they say they've been with
10) Anything that is coming out of their mouth
11) Around your sister, child or children, girlfriends, and family
12) Around your brother, child or children, homeboys, and family
13) To keep the promises they made to you
14) To do what they say they will do
15) To be who they say they are with
16) The key to your home
17) To pay a bill or help you pay bills
18) Your car
19) To get a job or stay on it
20) To change their life

Wow! The two of you are still in a marriage or relationship together! You say you love them and they say they love you, but you have these reason why you don't trust them. Wow! Why are you still with them? Are you afraid of being happy and alone? Or are you afraid to love yourself more than you love them? If you make a person a priority in your life and you are only an option in their life, then your priorities are all wrong.

KEEP YOUR DAMN MOTHER, FAMILY, AND FRIENDS OUT OF YOUR BUSINESS

The only person who should know what's going on in your home is the two people that live there. You should NEVER bring a third person into your marriage or relationship. If you are going to be together, then the two of you should find a way to communicate and work out any problem you may have. Think about this: you get mad and you call your mom in anger and tell her all these bad things about your man or woman. Then you two work out the problem and everything is going well. Now you wonder why mom is still mad at your man or woman. This is because you have painted a picture in her mind about this person and all the bad or mean things they are doing to you. Now she is mad at the man or woman all because of something you told her. So, now the two of you are lovie-dovie and your mom still dislikes this person and you don't know why. This is all because you put her in your business. Don't believe what people tell you about their relationship. People will give you advice about your relationship and their relationship is worse than yours. Remember, misery loves company.

THE SACRIFICES YOU MAKE FOR YOUR RELATIONSHIP

Sacrifices, we all make them for different reasons. Most of the time, that reason does not benefit you when it comes to your relationship. People make sacrifices for their relationship to keep them or to stay with a person. Some people will give up family, children, friends, a job, and a lot more just to be in a relationship with a person who doesn't want to be with them. Ask yourself, what have you sacrificed for your relationship? Was it worth it? What did the person you were with sacrifice for the relationship? What did they give up to be with you? Did your sacrifice change the course of your relationship? Did your sacrifice make the relationship better? Sometimes people sacrifice their happiness for someone else's happiness. If that is what you choose to do, then fine. Sacrifices are a very high price we pay and some of them can change your life or destroy your life. So before you make that ultimate sacrifice for a person, relationship, or marriage ask yourself: is this person truly worth it? Remember this: you can still have love in your heart for a person but not have that person in your life.

THREE THINGS THAT CAN AFFECT A RELATIONSHIP

Education: Ladies, most women are better educated than their man. This will play a big part in how your relationship will go. We as men think we know something about everything. When we meet a woman who challenges our knowledge, we have a problem with that. I will never tell a woman to dumb herself down just to be with a man. But some men have a problem with a well-educated and independent woman. Being well educated allows a woman to make more money than her man, which allows her to be more independent and self- sufficient than he is. Some men have a problem with that. Ladies, please do not be ashamed of or embarrassed about your education. If a man has a problem with that then you probably don't need him.

Economy: Due to the problems with the economy that we all face, there are lots of good men who find themselves unemployed through no fault of their own. The majority of men want to be good providers for their families. Unfortunately, bad things do happen to good men and sometimes a man will find himself out of a job. Ladies, there is nothing wrong with a man being unemployed, but there is a lot wrong with a man who chooses to stay unemployed. A real man will do whatever he has to do to provide for his woman and family. He will work more than one job if he has to. He will not allow his woman to be the sole provider for his family. He will do these things and many more because he knows that is what a real man should do for his woman and family. He will do these things because he knows his woman has his back. She will support and stand by him until he gets back on his feet.

Past Relationships: People, find out as much as you can about the past relationships of the person you choose to be with. You might choose a man who has been used to being taken care of by other women and expects for you to do the same. He expects for you to do the things that all the other women he has been with have done. This does not make him a bad man, this just means that this man has been with a lot of desperate and thirsty women. Ask yourselves why any man wouldn't want to work and do better when he has a woman that is willing to take care of him and meet his every need. Men, try to find out as much about the woman as you can. She might have trust issues from her last relationship because of cheating or abuse. This does not mean she will not trust you, but it does mean you will have to earn her trust and that might take a while. Let me give you a little advice. Sometimes you hold onto things that you know you should let go of. You do not want to accept the fact that you made a bad choice. You will stay with that decision, hoping that it will one day get better and it never does. When you have given this person all you have to give and they walk out on you, leaving you hurt, broken-hearted, and damaged, then you say there are no good men or women. All the time, you knew in your heart this person was not good for you from the start.

RELATIONSHIPS: ARE THEY WORTH THE TIME AND EFFORT?

I ask this question because I see people spending years in a relationship only to have it end and have to start a new one all over again. They are left wondering, "What happened? What could I have done better? Why did I stay so long?" Some relationships last a short time; some relationship last a long time. What the two have in common is they will end one day and usually not the way you would have wanted it to. Now you are left trying to pick up the pieces and piece back your life while the person you were with moves on with their life. I'm in no way downing relationships. I think they are great to be in, but only if you are in one with a person who is as committed to making it as successful as you are. Relationships are very hard and take a lot of work, effort, time, and commitment from two people - not just for the first months or year, but for the life of the relationship. Next to marriage, a relationship might be the second most common thing people commit to in their lives. People put more time and effort trying to make relationships work than they do anything else. Some people commit months and years of their lives trying to make a bad relationship better when it is easier just to walk away and cut your losses.

Ask yourself, why am I in my relationship? Am I happy with the person I'm with? Is the person I'm with happy with me? Is the person I'm with ready for a committed, exclusive relationship? How long have I been in this relationship? How long am I willing to stay in this relationship? Do I see this relationship going to the next step of marriage? Is the person I'm with the right person for me? Am I the right person for them? Are we the right people for each other? What do I want out of this relationship? What am I willing to put into it to get what I want?

Like I said, relationships are great to be in, but it takes work, time, and effort. Is what you put into one worth the reward you get out of it? Is it worth your time and effort to start a new relationship after the way the old one ended? Relationships, are they worth the time and effort?

<u>RELATIONSHIPS TAKE A PIECE OF YOU WHEN THEY END</u>

The majority of people who are in relationships are committed, are real about what they want out of them, and are willing to do whatever it takes to make them work. That can be a bad thing because every time a relationship ends, it takes a piece of you with it. The longer the relationship lasts, the bigger the piece it takes from you. When a relationship ends, that is bad enough. But when one ends in a way you did not expect, that really takes a piece of you - especially if you had put your all into trying to make it work. Relationships are hard enough on you just trying to make them work. When they end and you are left trying to figure out what happened or what went wrong, that can be traumatic. When you were in your relationships was the other person giving as much as you were giving? Some people give their all and receive nothing or not as much from the person they were with. Relationships do and will work out, but it takes two people working together for it to do so. If your relationship doesn't work out, remember this: when that person leaves you, they take a piece of you with them. When you do finally meet the right person, you may have nothing left to give them because you have given it away to all the other people you were in relationships with.

HOW MUCH EFFORT IS BEING PUT INTO YOUR RELATIONSHIP?

We can all agree that most relationships can be described by one of these percentages: 50-50, 60-40, or 80-20. Relationship will last or end on one of these percentages. Only you know where your relationship is and how much effort you and the person you are with are putting into it. For a relationship to work out, two people must work together for the good of the relationship. This can be difficult or nearly impossible to do if you and the person you are with are not on the same page when it comes to your relationship. I hear people say all the time that they gave 100% to their relationship and the other person didn't give half of that. That is because the other person was not as serious about the relationship as you were. Both people must be willing to commit and give 100% of their time to their relationship to make it work.

Some relationships last for years, but that does not make them good ones. Some relationships last for years and never lead to marriage. I have noticed that for some reason, the bad or dysfunctional relationships last the longest even though the two people are not getting anything positive out of it. For some reason, two people that don't need to be together will stay together.

Relationships, for whatever reason, bring people together. Sometimes people keep their relationship together for all the wrong reasons when they know they need to be apart. For some reason, bad and unhealthy relationships work for some people and that's why they stay in them. We all know someone who is in or has been in a bad or unhealthy relationship. Maybe you were in one or in one. Some of us stay in them for whatever reason. We know we are not getting what we need and we know the person we are with has not committed themselves to the relationship and is not taking it seriously. But we stay for months or years getting that 20 percent they put in while you are putting your 80 percent to make the relationship work. I guess 20 percent of a relationship is worth your time and effort?

ARE YOU IN TWO RELATIONSHIPS AND DON'T KNOW IT?

This is the case for most people. What I mean about this is that you have started a new relationship before you ended the old one. Let me explain. Some people move so fast when it comes to relationships that they are not really out of their old one before they are starting a new one. People start a new relationship while still trying to figure out what went wrong with the old one. They bring all that old hurt and pain into their new relationship. They bring those bad feelings and that mistrust into their new relationship. When it fails, you ask yourself why? Because you did not give yourself time to end that old relationship before you started a new one. Anytime a relationship ends, there are always questions about why the relationship ended. Sometimes you know the answer and sometimes you don't. If you have been in a relationship for years, you will have more questions than you do answers.

You must take this time to find out what went wrong and what you need to do better the next time. You must give yourself time to hurt, heal, and move on before you can start a new relationship. The longer the relationship lasts, the deeper the hurt will be when it is over and the longer the healing process will be. So don't deny yourself this process by trying to start a new relationship as soon as the old one is over. That is not fair to you or the new person you are with. You will only repeat the same mistakes and you must learn from your mistakes in order not to repeat them in the future. Mistakes will be made in a relationship and not all by the person you are with. You will also make mistakes. You must own up to your mistakes just like you want them to own up to theirs. A good relationship is the foundation of a great marriage to build upon. Remember, not all good boyfriends will make good husbands and fathers and not all good girlfriends will make good wives and mothers. By being in a relationship with a person, it helps you to determine if you want to be in a marriage with that person.

THERE ARE ALL TYPES OF RELATIONSHIPS

Before you enter into a relationship, you must first find what type of relationship you want to have with that person. What kind of relationship does that person want to have with you? There are all types of relationships. The one you have in mind may not be the same one the person you are with has in their mind. You might be thinking you are in an exclusive, one-on-one relationship, but the person you are with may not see it that way. This is why it is very important that you and the person you are with have an agreement on what type of relationship you are going to have. How many times have you thought you were in an exclusive relationship only to find out later the person you were with did not see it that way?

There are many types of relationships people enter into. Some of them can be misleading and you may find that out after you have spent months or years in it. The only why you can find out what type of relationship you are about to enter into is by talking with that person and coming to an agreement about the relationship. When you have done this, then both people must honor the terms of the agreement if the relationship is going to prosper and grow. Even with this agreement in place, most relationships will get off track at some point. This will happen when one or both people involved stop following the agreed upon terms. When this happens, most relationship will end - maybe not right away, but in time. People have to want a relationship to work. One person cannot make a relationship work.

Not all relationships are meant to be. Not all relationships will lead to marriage. Not all people that enter into a relationship are honest about what they want out of it. I look at relationships as a trial run before marriage. A good, healthy relationship just might lead to a good, healthy marriage. People do change and their needs change. You may one day need more from the person you are with. This is where most relationship fail. Both people need to be able to grow and change as the relationship grows and changes. If your relationship never changes, it will never grow. A relationship should evolve the longer you are in it. It should evolve in a positive way. If yours is not, ask yourself, what type of relationship am I in?

WHY GET MARRIED WHEN A RELATIONSHIP IS GOOD ENOUGH?

I ask this question because I see a lot of friends and family staying in relationships for 5, 10, 20, and 30 plus years. I thought a relationship was the next step to marriage. Ask yourself, how long must a relationship go on before marriage? Is the person you are with comfortable just been in a relationship? Are you comfortable just being in a relationship with that person? Is marriage not in your relationship plans? Do you feel like the person you are with is not marriage material? Does the person you are with feel like you are not marriage material? Are you good enough for a long-term relationship but not a long-term marriage?

I guess some people think a relationship is a substitution for marriage. If you stop and think about it, they might be right. Think about this: in most relationships, you have most if not all the benefits of a married person, but none of the obligations or commitments. You can have these benefits for 5, 10, 20, and 30 plus years. When you are tired or done with the relationship, you just walk away. The majority of the time, you leave without the legal problems that married couples have. I guess long term relationships do have their benefits. It benefits the person who does not want to go to the next level of marriage. When two people are in this type of relationship, one person might still be married or have some legal obligation to another person. Or they just might think you are good enough for a long-term relationship but not a long-term marriage. They may also wonder why they should buy the cow when they are getting the milk for free.

<u>WHY SOME RELATIONSHIPS DON'T WORK OUT</u>

There are thousands of reasons why relationships don't work out. We all know the most common reasons why. Cheating, being dishonest, lying, deceiving, the loss of trust, and the list goes on. But the main reason I think relationships don't work out is because two people should not be together in the first damn place. Ask yourself how many times you have been with a person that you knew you had nothing in common with you? Were you only with that person because of what they had, what they could do for you, or what they did to you? That's it! Other than those things, you and that person had nothing in common and nothing to build a successful relationship upon. We all have done this at one time or another and we call this a relationship. We do not put into it what we need to make it work, but we stay in the relationship for what we can get out of it. I said earlier, not all relationships are meant to be and not all people are meant to be together. But we will get with a person and stay with that person. Most of the time, we are unhappy, but we stay because the sex is good, the money is good, the benefits are good, we are comfortable, we don't want to move on, or we are afraid to move on and start a new relationship with a new person. We wonder why our relationship didn't work out? It's because it was not meant to be in the first place.

RELATIONSHIPS: ARE YOU READY FOR ONE?

I ask this question because I think we are all agree that a relationship takes work, effort, time, and commitment. Are you able to give yours all it needs in order to be successful? Relationships don't always end because a person gets caught cheating or they are not being honest. Sometimes they end because one or both people are just not capable of maintaining a healthy relationship. This can be due to mentally or physical disabilities. I'm not saying people with these disabilities cannot have a good functioning relationship, they can. But these disabilities must be discussed and addressed at the start of the relationship, not when there is a problem. Honesty and clarity with these issues at the start might help the relationship when they occur. Financial stability is another thing that must be in place before a relationship can be successful. You must be able to pull your part financially and your partner must be able to depend on you financially just as much as you depend on them. Relationships must be built on give and take not just give or take. This will never work in a functioning relationship.

THE KEPT RELATIONSHIPS

This is another common relationship where one person is taking care of another person for whatever reason. There is nothing wrong with this if the other person has some physical, mental, or health issues that prevent them from working or contributing financially to the relationship. This is not the case in most kept relationships. One person is just not working or doesn't want to work for whatever reason. The financial burden falls on the other person to carry the financial responsibilities in the relationship. In this kind of relationship, one person is not living up to their financial responsibility, but is living off their past accomplishments. For example, they might have been working at one time and were paying the bills or were helping to pay the bills. Or they may have come into some money at one time and were able to do more financially for the relationship than the other person. In any case, the person is living on their past accomplishments and feels they are justified in doing so. For some reason, the other person feels this is alright because they did help in the past, so one person assumes the full financial responsibility of the relationship. In some cases, a person will allow themselves to be kept just so they do not have to help out financially. This may mean the other person has to get a second source of income just to manage the bills. I have seen these relationships go on for years. One person is struggling to keep the relationship together financially and the other person is just enjoying the ride. The person that is supporting the relationship does this for months or years. They stay in this relationship even though they are not happy. They know they need to get out, but they stay hoping that things will change one day and the person they knew before will come back to them. I don't understand why a person stays in a relationship like this. I guess I will never know because I will never be in one. But if this is the way your relationship is, good luck with it! I only hope one day you will ask yourself: is this relationship worth the time, effort, and money that I am putting into it?

THE POWER OVER A PERSON

This is another type of relationship. A person will allow another person to stay or live with them and not contribute anything financially just to have that power over them. They know the person has no other place to go and must do as they say to continue to live there. This gives a person power over the other person. People like to be in control, and to be in control of another person's life is a power trip for some people. To have a person totally dependent on you for their livelihood is why some people allow a person to stay or live in their relationship without contributing anything to it.

What I am about to say next will upset and offend some of my female readers. But before you get mad at me, just think about your relationship and ask yourself, have you ever allowed a man to stay or live with you even though he is or was not contributing as much financially as you were? Some men are lazy, sorry, good-for-nothing bums. They will allow a woman to work, take care of them, and control some part of their lives just so they can stay at home and do nothing but watch T.V., movies, drink beer and alcohol, smoke weed, play video games, and have their homeboys over all day eating your food. That is okay if that is the kind relationship you allow him to have with you.

How many times have you stayed in a relationship out of obligation because of the things he did for you in the past when now he is unable to do them? How many times have you stayed in a relationship with a man because he was down on his luck or going through something? How many times have you felt he needs you to help him get back on his feet even though it's been months or years and he is still not able to contribute anything financially to the relationship? But you stay because of what he did for you in the past for you.

There is nothing wrong with helping a person, especially if you are in a relationship with that person. But ask yourself and be honest with yourself: is your help part of a plan to have some type of control over that person's life? By him living with you, you watch him and monitor his coming and goings. You know where he is at. He has to do what you want him to do when you want him to do it. Maybe you do not have total control, but you do have some control and that is good enough for you.

SEXLESS RELATIONSHIPS

I don't understand this type of relationship at all. How can you live with a person and not have any or some sexual or physical attraction to them? I don't understand how you can be in the same house with a person and not want them to touch you. How you can be in the same house and not sleep in the same bed? How you can be in the same house and hate the sight of the person you are living with? How you can live with a person when you are not happy? I hear this from people that are in these sexless relationships. My question to them is what did a person do to you to make you want to stop having sex with them? I got many answers, such as they were cheating, they could not be trusted, or they were not who they said they were. I asked, knowing all of that, why don't you just leave and find someone that you can have sex with?

Sex is not everything in a relationship, but it is one of the things that make a relationship fun to be in. I asked a lot of questions about sexless relationships and got a lot of different answers. None of them made sense to me, but I guess it makes all the sense in the world to the people who stay in sexless relationships for months or years. I would think if the people I was in a relationship did not find me sexually or physically attractive, one of us would have to leave. The time and effort is just not worth what you put in it. You can be in a sexless relationship by yourself. Why be in one with a person you are in a relationship with?

LOVELESS RELATIONSHIPS

For the life of me, I do not understand how two people can be in a relationship and not be in love. It happens more than people like to admit. People are in relationships with a person that they don't love. Why are you in a relationship with a person that has told you or showed you that they do not love you? Why are you with a person that you have told you don't love them? In writing this book, I talked to many people about their relationships and how they feel about them. We agreed on one thing; relationships are great to be in if the two people in them are equally committed to each other. I asked what happens when the commitment is not there by the other person. Is it time to leave the relationship and move on? I got more excuses than answers. People gave more excuses as to why they should stay than reasons why they should leave. I am not judging anyone on how they live their life. But for me, I want a person in my life that loves me as much as I love them. We all know people who are in or have been in these loveless relationships.

Someone reading this book might be in that type of relationship. If you are, ask yourself why? Why are you with a person who does not love you as much as you love them? Why are you with a person who continues to hurt you and disrespect you? Why are you with a person who you can see you have no future with? Why are you in love with a person when you know they are in love with someone else? Why do you love a person who doesn't love themselves? How can you love a person who mistreats you? How can you continue to give a person your love when they have proven to you time and time again that they are not worthy of your love?

I wonder if people today are so desperate for love or to be loved that they will give their love to a person knowing that person does not love them. Do people today want to be in a relationship so bad that it makes no difference if the person they love does not have any love for them? Are relationships without love still relationships? How can you love a person that continues to say mean and hateful things to you? How can you love a person that continues to break your heart? How can you love a person that you can't trust? How can you love a person that cheats on you? How can you love a person that beats and abuses you? I guess it is easy to love this person when you don't love yourself. There is an old saying, "Love is a splendid thing." It may be, but one thing I know is that love, in most relationships, is blind.

DO YOU HAVE A PLAN FOR YOUR RELATIONSHIP'S FUTURE?

If you are in a relationship, take a minute and think about this: how long have you been in that relationship and where is it going? What is the future of your relationship? Will this relationship lead to marriage? Will a child be born into this relationship? Was that child planned for? Was the relationship ready for that child? Was that relationship suitable for that child to be in? What do you expect from your relationship? Is your relationship living up to your expectations?

People spend years of their lives in a relationship or trying to make one work. In the end, they find out that it was not worth the time and effort they put into it. So, the relationship never grows and has no future. Did you plan for the relationship that you are in now? Did you have a plan in place for your last relationship? Do you have a plan for any future relationships? Most people just start a relationship without a plan. They just hope it will work out and everything will be okay. Before you start a relationship, you must have a plan in place. You must know what you are willing to put in it and you must know what you want out of it. You must try to find someone who is as compatible with you as you are with them. You must find someone that is looking for some of the same things you are looking for in a relationship. You must find someone that you can communicate with and who knows how to communicate with you.

Good looks and good sex is no reason to start a relationship. They are fun, but if that's the only reason you want to be with a person, then man or woman up and tell the person you are with why you are with them. If you are in a relationship with a person just because they look good or the sex is good, then there is nothing wrong with that person - there is something wrong with you. One day, the looks will change and sex will get old. Then what do you have? A relationship with a person that you can't stand to look at and one with a person you don't want to have sex with anymore. You find yourself in a relationship with an ugly person that you don't want to have sex with and a relationship that has no future.

THE DRAMA-FILLED, DYSFUNCTIONAL, AND UNHEALTHY RELATIONSHIP

People want what they can't handle or what they don't need. People enter into drama- filled, dysfunctional, and unhealthy relationships knowing they have no business being with that person. They think they can change them or handle the drama in that person's life. When they realize they can't, they don't know how to get out or they are too deeply involved to leave. They are stuck in that unhealthy relationship with all that drama and dysfunction with a person they know they should not have been with in the first place. They continue to stay and be unhappy rather than try to find a way out or be honest with that person and tell them they want out of the relationship. The longer they stay, the more normal that drama-filled, dysfunctional, and unhealthy relationship becomes to them. They start to believe this is the way relationships are supposed to be, so they stay. Some have lived a life filled with drama and dysfunction. When they meet a person with the same things going on in their lives, they are drawn to that person. They will stay with that person for months and years because they feel their relationship is normal and they are afraid to seek out anything better.

HAVE YOU CONVINCED YOURSELF TO STAY?

People stay in bad or meaningless relationships all the time. For whatever reason, they just won't get out or move on. They keep talking themselves into staying or keep coming up with reasons why they should not leave. I don't understand. If you are not happy with a person, why stay with that person? If a person is not happy being with you, why do they stay? Ask yourself: is your relationship where it should be? If not, how much longer are you going to give it to get there? Do you or the person you are with have any plans for the future growth of your relationship? Why is it taking so long to get to that point? What hold does that person have you? What are they doing to you or for you to make you stay when you know you should leave? Is whatever you getting from them worth your happiness? Do you stay because of a child or children? Do you stay because you are afraid to leave? Do you stay for the comfort or convenience? Do you stay because you have years invested in the relationship? Are you afraid to move on and start a new life alone? Are you afraid the other person will find someone better than you to be with? Are you afraid you cannot support yourself on your own? Are you afraid nobody else wants you because of your looks, weight, or age? Are you just use to the way that person treats you? Are you ashamed to leave because of what people might say about you? Are you ashamed to leave after all time you have put in this relationship? Whatever the reason you stay in your relationship is yours, but if you are not happy and your relationship has no future, why are you still in it? You must convince yourself to leave the same way you convince yourself to stay.

FRIENDSHIPS VS. RELATIONSHIPS

People, let's stop playing with each other's feelings. If you are with a person and you only want a friendship with that person, please let them know. If you only want a friend with benefits, please let that person know. Don't have them thinking that they are in relationship when you know that is NOT what you want. Stop wasting their time and yours by leading them on, having them thinking that they are in a relationship when they are not. If you are in a relationship and you feel that it has run its course, please tell the other person. Please find the words and courage to tell them it's over! Yes! You might hurt their feelings, but how do you think they would feel after months and years with you and then you tell them that you've been unhappy for those months and years? It's okay to enjoy being around a person and liking the things that you do together, and even how that person makes you feel. This does not mean that you are in a relationship with this person. No matter how much you want it to be, if the person you are with is not willing to take it to the next level, it will remain a friendship and not a relationship.

RELATIONSHIPS: THE GOOD, THE BAD, AND THE UGLY

Relationships: there are three kinds. Let's see which one you are in.

- *The Good Relationship:* This relationship is when two people find each other and decide they want to make it an exclusive relationship. They know that a good relationship takes hard work, trust, honesty, understanding, communication, respect, and love. They are willing to work together to achieve all of these things. They know that these things will not come overnight, but are willing to put in hard work so that one day they will be able to have a long, happy relationship and life together. They also know that when someone loves you, they don't have to say a word. You can tell by the way they treat you.

- *The Bad Relationship:* This kind of relationship is when two people are together for comfort and convenience. They are not willing to work to make the relationship better. They have lost interest in each other and there is no communication, commitment, respect, or trust. There is no attraction physically or sexually. There is no affection or desire to be shared. However, they stay in this relationship for convenience, comfort, and due to the fear of moving on. They know all along that this relationship is over and done, but neither one of them wants to be the first say goodbye.

- *The Ugly Relationship:* This relationship happens when two people know that they do not need to be together. They know there is nothing left for him or her. This relationship has become abusive mentally, physically, and verbally. It's toxic! Both parties know that the relationship has run its course, but they stay in this relationship for months and years. They feel like there is nowhere to go and there is no one else that would want them. This relationship must end. It's in the best interest of both parties to walk away before one or both ends up hurt or dead.

Out of these three relationships, which one are you in? I hope that you are in number one and that it is going well. I hope that you and your partner are very happy together and you two are working together to make the relationship grow. If it is number two and it can't be worked out, it's okay to leave. Life is too short. Don't spend months or years with a person that you have lost interest in and no longer want to be with. Sometimes, relationships just don't work out and it is time to move on. Remember, a person doesn't miss you when you are gone, they miss you when you have moved on.

If it is number three, please, somebody leave this relationship! Remember, a relationship is more than finding the right person; it's being the right person. One person cannot be in a relationship by themselves. It takes two people working together to make it work. So if you are not ready to totally commit yourself to another person, you are not ready to be in a relationship.

DON'T BE IN A CAREER RELATIONSHIP

Some relationships are like careers. People start them and stay in them, knowing they are not going anywhere and are never going to advance to the next level of marriage. Every relationship should lead to something, hopefully marriage. Isn't that why you are in yours? Or are you in it just to say you have one?

Ladies, think about your relationship and about the problems you are having in it. I bet you will see your problems are not new ones. They are the same old ones you have been having for months or years. Now think about your last marriage or relationship and why or how it ended. Now ask yourself, was it because of some new problems that came up? Or was it because of the same old problems that you have been dealing with for months and years? Now ask yourself, why were you two not able to resolve those problems or prevent them from happening over and over again? There is a reason for this and I will tell you about it later.

What I will tell you now is that for a relationship to work, both people in it have to want it to work. To be honest with you, most men, not all, do not want to be with the woman he is with. However, he still needs her for his own personal reasons. This is because most of the time, the woman that a man is with is not the woman he truly wants to be with. Even if you are his wife, you may not be the woman he truly wants in his life. Ladies, you may believe just because you are the woman he married or is in a relationship with, you are the women he wants to be with. Not true! Why did he stay with me for all those years? Why was he telling me he loved me and he didn't? Why didn't he just go be with the woman he loved or wanted to be with? Why did he put me through all of that hell when he could have just left? Ladies, ask yourself this: if he loves you as much as he says, why does he continue to break your heart, abuse you, disrespect you, and lie to you while he is telling you he loves you? I will answer those questions and many more. Ladies, the majority of men choose a woman because he knows she is the best thing for him. He knows the happiness and joy she can bring into his life. But some men choose a woman for what she do can for him.

WHY HE CHOSE YOU

We as people believe that the person we chose to be in our lives, whether through marriage or relationships, feel the same way about us as we feel about them. But when it comes to most men, ladies, you are so wrong about that. I listed the four reasons why men marry or entered into relationships with a woman. This does not mean all men think like this, but ladies, think about the man you are with or were with. Why is he with you? The reasons he is with you are money, sex, lodging, and food. I am not saying that these are the only reasons that a man gets with a woman. But men know that by being with a woman, she will have one or all of these things in her life. She will gladly share them with the man that she has chosen to be with. For this reason, I say your man has chosen to be with you, not because you are his best choice, but because you can provide him with the things he needs most: money, sex, lodging, and food.

Now men do marry women and enter into relationships with them because she is truly the woman he loves. Ladies, if you are blessed to have a man that chose you for you and not because of what you have or what you can do for him, then good for your marriage or relationship. But if you chose a man that is constantly lying, cheating, disrespecting, and abusing you, you are not the woman that he chose to be with even if he stays with you. Let's break these four things down and see why your man chose you.

Money: In today's society, women are better educated and can get a better job or career than most of the men she marries or enters into a relationship with. Most women are independent, strong-minded, and do not need a man to support them or take care of them. However, they would love to share their lives with the right man. Ladies, ask yourself, when you met your man or husband, who had the better education - you or him? Most men know he is not on your level as far as education goes, but he looks at this as a way to get the things he wants without spending his money on them. Women, you are kind, helpful, trusting, devoted, and committed to making you marriage or relationship work. You do everything you can to make sure your husband or man has what he needs, even if sometimes, you just can't afford it. But you will always find a way to provide for him because that's the way women are. Ladies, ask yourself, in the marriage or relationship you are in now, whose yearly income is bigger - yours or your man's? Ask yourself, who is responsible for the majority of the bills getting paid - you or your man? If your man is the one that is paying the majority of the bills, did it start off that way? Is it that way now? Did the marriage or relationship end that way? Now ask yourself, why did he choose me? Not all men chose a woman for what he can get out of her. But ladies, ask yourselves this after being with this man for months or years: why did he choose me? Ladies, are you getting out as much as you are putting in to your marriage or relationship? Or did you get as much out of your marriage or relationship as you put in it? Choice number one: your money.

Lodging: Most women, when a man meets her, already has her own place to live. She can afford it or she is providing a place for her and her child or children to live. Most men, not all men, know this. This is why some men chose to be with a woman that he really doesn't want to be with. Ladies, I know you might be saying I'm wrong. You might not even want to own up to the fact that you once had or have a man in your life because he has no other place to go. Let's be real about this. The majority of the time, as a relationship goes on, you may notice he is spending more time at your place than you are spending at his. There are cases when you meet a man and he does have his own place free from kids, family, and friends. You will find yourself at his place, but not as much as he is at yours for whatever the reason. Ladies, ask yourselves, how many men have you met that had his own place free from kids, family, and friends? How many men have you met that lived alone? A man not having his own place does not make him a bad man, a bum, or lazy, but it does make his choice of you a lot easier because you have your own place.

Ladies, think about this: How many of you know a woman that has had a man move in with her when the relationship starts to progress? How many times have you been with a man and you moved in with him? How many times has your man moved in with you? When you and your man moved in together, did he have his own place to move you into? Did you move him into your place? Did you move in with his mother, friend, or family member? The truth is, the majority of the time when a man and a woman make the decision to live together, the man will usually move in with the woman. Even with it being her place, she will gladly share it with the man she chose to be with. A man knows that and that is why he chose you. Choice two: you have you own place.

Food: With a job and a place to stay, your man knows he will always eat because you have to eat. Even if he is not contributing as much of the food as you are, he still eats. He knows that as long as you and your kids eat, he will also eat. Because it is your food, you gladly share it with him because you chose him. That is what women do and that's why he chose you. Choice three: your food.

Sex: Ladies, what can I say about that? Ladies, you own all of that but you gladly share it with the man you chose. That's what women do and that is why your man chose you. Choice four: your sex.

Ladies I am not saying all men choose a woman for these four things. Most men do love the woman he married or is in a relationship with. But ask yourself, what has your man brought to the table?

WHO CHOSE WHOM?

Ladies, ask yourself did the man choose to be with you or did you make the choice for the both of you? Think about your marriage or relationship you are in now if your husband or man could get out of it would he? If he could get a do over do you think he will still choose you to marry or be in a relationship with? Do you think you were his first choice to be in a marriage or relationship with? Why do you think your husband or man chose you? Were you the only choice he had? Men choose to be with woman for a lot of reason and most of the time their reason are not for the same reason women choose to be with a man. Most men choose to be with a woman for lots of reason and most of the time it does not benefit the woman he is with. When a man chose to be with a woman chances are, he has learned all he needs to know about her and how she will act to certain situations that may come up in the marriage or relationship. So, he tests her not by doing something big like cheating of beating her but by doing something small that she will not notice, such as stop helping with the bills, not being available when his woman needs him or change his routine and habits for no reason. Some men do choose to prey on women and some women choose to allow a man to prey on them maybe that is the reason why your man chose you?

LADIES, CAN WE TALK?

You are in control of your life and nothing will happen unless you allow it to happen. There will not be date if you don't allow it, there would be no relationship if you don't allow it and there will be no marriage if you don't say yes. You have the power over your life and you control how you should be treated. Just because you get married or in a relationship does not mean you have to give over your power. Ladies you are strong, independent, intelligent, and confident you do not need a man to define you. You can make it through life with a man or without a man. But some of you when you get with a man you give him the power over your life and that is why he beats you cheat on you, disrespect and abuse you. You must take back your power by doing this you will take back your life. These are things that might help you to make better choices when it comes to choosing a man to date be in a relationship or marry. Your life is yours to control and NOT anyone else.

LADIES, COMMUNICATION IS THE KEY.

Ladies, communication is the foundation that you should build your relationship upon. There are lots more, but this should be number one. Another mistake you make when you are looking for a man is rushing into a relationship before you truly get to know and learn all you can about him. You will spend more time and effort trying to catch that man cheating than trying to find out if he is a cheater before you got with him. I hear a lot of you say after a break up, "I didn't know that about him," "I didn't think he would do that," or "I didn't see that coming." If you would just talk to your man, listen to what he is telling you. It just might save you a lot of hurt and pain.

Ladies, ask questions and demand answers. How can you have a successful relationship with a man when you hardly know anything about him or you can't communicate with him? Before you start a relationship, get everything out in the open. Find out his likes, his dislikes, his do's and his don'ts, what he will do and won't do, and make damn sure you find out as much as you can about him. This will be your only chance you may have to talk to your man about these things. After you enter into a relationship with him, it will be hell to talk about these things. Ask questions about his life and plans for the future. Are you in them? Is he looking for a serious relationship or friends with benefits? What is his sexual preference? Does he like men or women? Does he like regular one-on-one sex or does he want other women to join in?

Ladies, don't be afraid to ask these questions and many more. I have been asked these questions and many like them by ladies and it didn't offend me or make me mad. I want to be a real man who doesn't have anything to hide. Ask these questions now so you will not have to find out the answers to them later. Try to find out as much as possible about the man you are about to allow in your life and your child or children's lives. Remember, you are in control of your own life. Nothing can happen unless you allow it to happen. Please choose wisely!

WHAT YOU SEE IS WHAT YOU GET; SEEING IS BELIEVING

Ladies, how many times have you heard those old sayings? How many times have you said it yourself? But you still don't believe what you see when it comes to choosing a man. You ignore the fact that this man might not be the right man for you. Is this man a good choice for you? There are good men out there, but some of you just keep choosing the wrong man. You see a man for what you want him to be, not for who he is.

A lot of you say these words, "I can see the good and the potential in him." "I can change him." A lot of you try to bring the best out of him. Ladies, if he can't see it for himself, if he is unwilling to try to change and do better, then you are wasting your time and energy. A man will only change if and when he wants to. It is sad, but a lot of you ladies are finding that out the hard way, after you have given him months and years of your life and he is still the same bum he was when you first met him.

Ladies, yes! You should stand by your man and you should help and support your man, but you should have a time limit. If he loses his job and is out of work for any given reason, give him a time limit to find, fix, or correct the problem. A man that loves his wife, woman, and family will do all he can to take care of them and provide for them. If your husband or man is not doing this thing, it may be time to move on. Ask yourself, if you stop cooking, cleaning, taking care of yourself and the family, giving him all that good freaky sex he likes, what do you think he will do? You all know the answer. He will leave you and find someone who will.

Ladies, the Bible tells you if a man doesn't work, then he doesn't eat. A man will earn his living by the sweat of his brow, not by the sweat of his wife of woman's brow. The dictionary explains the definition of insanity it is to keep doing the same thing over and over and expect a different result. That's what a lot of you ladies are doing when it comes to choosing a man. You keep doing the same thing and going about it the same way, yet you expect a different result. You know why you keep finding "Mr. Wrong" because you keep looking for "Mr. Right Now!" You are looking for "Mr. Right" in all the "wrong places." Stop settling for less. Stop undervaluing yourself. Know yourself worth. Make sure your man lives up to your expectations and stop trying to live up to his. Demand better for yourself and stop settling for less.

Some of you say things like, "He will change," "I can change him," "He will never do that to me," and "He just needs someone to stand by him, help him, and have his back." Ladies, let me share something with you. A real man knows when he needs to make a change in his life. A real man will make that change and he will make sure it's in a positive way. A real man will treat a woman like he would treat his own mother, sister, and daughter. A real man knows his woman's worth. He knows she is not there to take care of him, but she will help him, support him, and stand by his side. A real man knows the value of having a good woman in his life. He will do everything in his power to make sure she knows that she is loved, appreciated, and needed. He will let her know that being with her completes him. Ladies, if you don't see these qualities in your man, then once again, you have chosen the wrong man.

BAD CHOICES WILL LEAD TO A BAD LIFE

Ladies, we all make bad choices in life. We make bad choices with our finances, jobs, career, friends, and the way we chose to live our lives. But we make the necessary changes to fix these problems. When you make a bad choice in choosing a man, most women choose to live with that bad choice and be unhappy rather than make a change and be happy. I don't understand. Women, when you go shopping and you make a bad choice in shoes or a dress, you take them back and get something that pleases you. But when you make a bad choice in a man, you act like there is no exchange policy. All sales are final you are stuck with him for life. You don't remove this problem from your life. You say things like, "It will get better," "I can deal with it," and, "He will change." I don't understand. You will take back a pair of shoes that hurt your feet; you will take back a dress that doesn't fit you right. But you will keep this bad choice of a man in your life, even when you know he means you no good.

This is the man you give your best years to. This is the man you allow to dog you out, beat you, and disrespect you. When he has done all these things to you and leaves you broken-hearted, damaged, and used up, then you say there are no good men out there. All because you made a choice and didn't do anything to fix it. I say to you that there are good men out there, you just chose to keep the bad ones in your life.

LADIES, ASK FOR MORE AND DEMAND MORE

Ladies, only you know what you are looking for in a man. Only you can make the decision on what kind of man you will allow into your life. Ask yourself, are you basing your decision about a man on your needs or wants? Be honest with yourself and the man you choose to let in your life and into your child or children's lives. Remember, not all good boyfriends will make good husbands. Not all good husbands will make good fathers. It is up to you to choose. So please choose wisely and be honest with yourself about your choices. Here are a few things that I suggest you look for in choosing a man:

1) His work ethic and views on life.
2) The kind of relationship he has with the women in his life, such as his mother, sister, or daughter.
3) His morals and values and how are they when it comes to family.
4) His relationship with God.
5) His education and ability to solve problems.
6) His ability to talk to you and communicate with you.
7) His ability to learn and try new things.
8) His ability to express love to you and others.
9) His ability to trust and forgive.

The most important thing of all:

10) Does this man even want to be in a relationship with you?

Ladies, the biggest mistake you make is thinking a man wants you just because he is with you. That is not always true. Ladies these are my ten things I think you should know when it comes to choosing a man. There are many more, but only you know what you are looking for in a man.

LET'S TALK ABOUT SEX

Ladies, please establish a VERY CLEAR UNDERSTANDING about what you will do to him sexually and what you will not do to him sexually before the relationship gets started. Get a VERY CLEAR UNDERSTANDING of what he can do to you sexually and what he cannot do to you sexually before the relationship gets started. Most men, not all men, have fantasies about having a threesome (you know, being with you and other women at the same time). There is nothing wrong with this; we all have our own fantasies. But ladies, it's fine if you are not okay with this. Let him know up front so there will be no MISUNDERSTANDING LATER. You must be up front and honest about what you will and will not do sexually and what you will allow and not allow in the relationship. Stand strong about what you say. Say what you mean and mean what you say. If he is a real man that respects all women, he will understand and respect you and what you have told him. If he doesn't agree to it then he was not the man for you. Move on. You will find the right man for you.

LADIES, REAL MEN RESPECT REAL WOMAN

Ladies, real men respect real women. You might ask what, does he mean by that? Some men would love to have a weak woman to take care of him, give him money, sex, a place to live, and allows him to stay at home while she goes to work. He doesn't want anything out of life. Now he knows he has a woman that thinks the same way he does and that makes him very happy. He knows he can say or do anything to you and you are okay with it just as long as he stays with you. He knows he does not have to respect you or treat you right. He knows all he has to do is just be with you and that will make you happy.

Ladies, a real man knows when he has a real woman because he will treat her with LOVE and RESPECT. He knows he will get the same from her. He will cherish her and let her know how much her love means to him. He will make sure she has the things she needs to make her life better. She does not have to tell him what she needs. He will know because he knows what kind of woman he has. He knows having her in his life makes his life better. He knows that after she has paid her bills, she might need his help financially. He will gladly give it to her because he knows she would do the same for him. A real man would never ask his woman to do anything that she feels uncomfortable, ashamed, or embarrassed doing. He would never ask her to put aside her morals or values just to satisfy him or his sexual desires. He knows his woman is independent and don't need him to take care of her, but she allows him in her life and will share it with him. He thanks God for her every day. He shows her and tells her all the time how much better his life is now that she is in it. Ladies, is this your man? Is he a real man? If not, then why are you with him?

LADIES, YOU ARE QUEENS

To the lady that is sleeping with and running around with your best friend's husband, your sister's husband, and maybe your mother's husband: I hear women say that their bodies are their temples. It is something to be respected and treasured. Well, let me ask you this: how many men do you let drive your car? Now, how many men have you allowed in your temple or let have your body? If your body is a temple and a temple is sacred, then why are you allowing men to violate it? You need to stop all of that madness! Change your life; you are better than that. You are a Queen, and a Queen only sleeps with one King. Remember this: you can't do what the men do and still call yourself a lady. Refuse to be his side piece, jump off, lady on the side, side chick, or booty call baby. You are better than that and you deserve better! Stop being his sometime, his down time, his maybe time. If he can't be there for you all the time, then he is not worth your time.

Ladies, the best way to be treated with respect is to DEMAND it and accept nothing less. Quit falling for the lies he is telling you about what his woman or wife is not doing for him, to him, or the things he says he needs done. You fall for his lies about that good, strong woman that he has at home. The reason why she is not doing all those things is because he is not being the man she needs him to be. His wife is a strong woman with values and morals. She is not going to put up with all his mess, so he comes to you because he knows that you are weak, have low self-esteem, and no respect for yourself. You have no morals or values. He knows you will fall for his lies. You will do all of those freaky, crazy things that his strong wife or woman won't do. He knows that you are a weak-minded woman and desperate to have a man, any man. Therefore, he uses you. When he is done, he goes back to that strong wife or woman that he really loves. You are left all alone, hurt, confused, and feeling used. Stop being that desperate woman. Please take your time and find someone that will treat you right and love you like he should.

MEN, CAN WE TALK?

Men, what is your definition of a good woman? What is your definition of your ideal woman? Do you know the difference between the two? I know this is a man's world, but it's not anything without a woman or a girl. Brothers, good women come in all shapes, sizes, and colors. What you see on the outside does not make her a good woman on the inside. If you have a good woman and she is treating you right, and she is doing all the things that she needs to do to keep you happy, please help her. Stand by her. Treat her with love, respect, and honor. She does all these thing and more for you.

MEN, PLEASE HELP YOUR WIFE, WOMAN, OR BOO FINANCIALLY

Guys, if she is doing all of the things that you need to keep you happy, please help her! You know if she has children, she needs help financially. Help her with the gas, lights, rent, groceries and/or daycare. It's okay to pay a bill or two. She is trying to take care of these things on her own, along with trying to keep you happy.

Men, you are with this woman. You live with her; you sleep with her. Yet when she asks you for a penny, you say that you don't have any. When she asks you for a dime, you whine. If she asks you for a dollar, you want to holler. This is your wife, your girlfriend, your woman, your boo, your baby, so help her. You know that her paycheck will only go so far. Open your wallet and give her some money. After all, you call her your woman. I'm not saying to make her bills your bills, but you know when she falls short financially, she should not have to ask or beg you for help.

Men, pay your child support like the courts ordered you to do. That money is not for her. It is for your children. I know you think that she is not doing the things that she should do with the money, but you know, it's okay. That is between her and her God. You just do what you have to do, and send the money every month on time.

MEN, PLEASE BE A PART OF YOUR CHILD'S LIFE

Men, please be a part of your child's life. Take up time with them even if you can't do for them financially. Giving your kids your time. It will go a long way with strengthening your relationship with your kids. I know. I was a young father at the age of 25. I had four kids by two different women and all my kids were under the age of six. I was not always able to do for them financially, but I would always give my time. I would pick them up and take them to and from school, help them with homework, and take them to their doctor and dentist appointments. I went to their sports events and school functions. I would get them on the weekends so their moms could go out for a lady's night or for a date. You can be in your kid's life without being in their mother's life. Your life will be better for this. If she is your "Baby," help your "Baby" when she needs you to. Remember, men, the strength of a man is not in how many women he can love, but how well you can love the woman you are with.

HOW DID YOU GET YOUR LADY: BY LYING, SCHEMING, AND BEING DISHONEST?

The same thing it took to get your baby is going to take the same thing to keep her. So if you got your lady by lying, you are going to have to keep on lying to keep her. If you got her by buying her, you are going to have to keep on buying. If you got her by scheming and being dishonest, you've got to keep on scheming and being dishonest.

Men, the way you got that woman and entered into the relationship with her is the way she will expect it to be. Don't get mad at her when you are no longer able to keep up that lie and front. The day that she finds out who you truly are and leaves you, remember - you went into this relationship with that lie on your tongue. I can tell you this: in all of my years of dealing with all types of women, I've never met a bad one. I've met a lot of good women who have gone bad. Most of the time it is because of what some man has done to her.

So let's man up to our women. Let's be husbands and fathers. Let's be the man of our homes because our women are tired of holding down that job for us! When she does something to make you mad (and she will), don't hit her. Give her a hug. When she says something that makes you mad, don't hit her in the mouth, kiss her on the lips. If you feel that you have to put your hands on her, make sure it is only to hold, caress, and make sweet love to her. Remember, men, all of us have mothers, sisters, and daughters. Think about this! What would you do if a guy was beating, abusing, and mistreating them? Go look at that man in the mirror; that man is you! Lastly, remember this: most of the time, it's cheaper to keep her. If you treat that woman like she is worthless, another man will come along and show her that she is priceless.

MEN: WHY DON'T WE TREAT THAT GOOD WOMAN RIGHT

Men, we spend all of our lives praying to God to help us find a good lady. When we do find her, what do we do? We lie to her, cheat on her, beat and abuse her, and we don't treat her right. We disrespect her. When she has taken all the mess that she can take, she leaves us. Then what do we do? We want to kill her and make her life a living hell. So I say to all of you, if you are blessed to find a good woman, stop doing all that mess you are doing. Leave your homeboys in the streets, leave that club life, and leave all those women that you are chasing alone. Get a job, and take care of your woman and your children. Love your woman, tell her that you love her, honor and protect her, keep her safe, and show her just how much you cherish her. Let her know that she completes your life. Tell her how much you need her in your life. Make her feel like she is very special to you. Be the father to your children and be the husband or man that your wife or woman always knew you were. If you do these things, I know you will have a woman that will stand beside you when times are good or bad.

MEN AND WOMEN: HERE ARE 10 QUESTIONS

Answer Them Truthfully to See How You Feel About Your Relationship:

1) Would you have sex with your partner without a condom or protection?   Yes or No
2) Do you look forward to making love to your partner?   Yes or No
3) Would you make your partner the beneficiary of your life insurance policy?   Yes or No
4) Do you miss the person you are with when they are gone?

          Yes or No

5) If you could get a do-over, would you still be in a committed relationship with the same person?

                              Yes or No

6) Would you give the person you are with access to your money or bank account?   Yes or No

7) Is your relationship where you thought it would be at this stage or time?   Yes or No

8) Do you think the person that you are in a relationship with is as committed to making it work as you are?

                              Yes or No

9) Does the person that you are with ever tell you how much they love you or how happy you make them?

                              Yes or No

10) Are you in love with the person that you are with, or do you just love the person that you are with?

                              Yes or No

How many questions do you have where you answered yes?

_____

How many questions do you have where you answered no?

_____

MY THOUGHTS ABOUT RELATIONSHIPS

Relationships are good to be in if you are with the right person, but they do take hard work to make them work. The best relationships are the ones where two people can communicate and work though their problems. This relationship has no lying, cheating, abuse of any kind, and no disrespect. It is filled with love, trust, honesty, caring, and respect. Both people can communicate and work out any problems they may have. The two people in this relationship have a plan for their future, have set goals, and are working hard to reach them. They know the road will not be easy. There will be obstacles and challenges, but they know by working together, they can overcome anything. They know that neither one is perfect and both will make mistakes. However, they both try to learn from them and not keep repeating the same mistakes. They are a team. Both are able to express their own opinions and all decisions are made by both. They work together for the better of the relationship and own up their obligations and financial responsibilities. They are both considerate of each other's feeling, needs, and desires. They only want the best for each other and for the relationship. They both plan for that next step of marriage and all that comes with it. They know it will be a little frightening and challenging, but by working together, they know they can overcome anything. These are my thoughts about relationships; you have your own. I hope things work out for you. Like the title of the book says, relationships: are they worth the time and effort? Is yours?

LADIES HERE IS SOMETHING FOR YOUR SPRIT

I hear you say you are praying and asking God for a church-going man and a God-fearing man. There is nothing wrong with that. Now ask yourself, is the man you are with or were with - a God-fearing man a church-going man? Or did he go to church with you only sometimes? Did that change the way he treated you and your marriage or relationship with him? So you have or had the man in your life that you are praying to God for - how is that working out for you? If I may suggest, change up what kind of man you pray and ask God for. Instead of praying for a church-going man and a God-fearing man, why don't you ask for a man that has a relationship with God? Ask for a man that has committed his life to severing Him. If he has a commitment with God, then he will be committed to you. Be blessed!

THANK YOU FOR YOUR SUPPORT
Thank You God, My Father

I would like to thank God for watching over me when I was out in the world doing things I had no business doing. I knew if it wasn't for your grace, mercy, favor and blessings, I would have been dead either by someone's hand or HIV or AIDS.

THANK YOU MOM; I LOVE YOU SO MUCH

I'd like to thank the most wonderful mother of all time. Even though you are not with us now, the love I have for you is as strong as the love you had for me. I know I kept you on your knees praying to God to look over me and keep me safe. I knew the only reason I am still alive is because of your special relationship you had with God. I knew when your prayers reached God's ears, He would listen and look down on you and say, "No, not Randy again!" Mom, I may not have been the best child you had, but you were the greatest Mother a boy could ask for. Even though you are with God now, I bet you are still worrying God to look after Randy.

THANK YOU, BISHOP AND PASTOR WILLS

I'd like to thank my little sister, Pastor Linda Willis and her husband, Bishop Kevin Willis. They knew my lifestyle and they never judged me. I was always welcome in their home and church.

A VERY SPECIAL THANKS TO PASTOR LINDA WILLIS

I would like to give a very special thanks to my Pastor Linda Willis. Over the years, you have been more to me than a sister. You have been my psychiatrist, spiritual advisor, life coach, and the person I told all of my dark secrets to - and there were a lot. You listened to me and you guided me though all of that madness I had going on in my life and you never charged me. Thanks. I love you, Little Sister.

THANK YOU, FAMILY

I would like to thank my family for always telling me, "Boy, you need to get some Jesus in your life." I did and I thank you.

LAST BUT NOT LEAST

To the little old-school, church-going lady that lived under me in my apartments. She would see me bringing all those women up and down the stairs at all times of the day and night. Thank you. You never said a word to me. All you did was stand there with your arms folded, shaking your head from side to side and say to me, "Son, I am praying for you." Thank you and may God Bless you all.

LOOK FOR MY BOOKS ON MY WEBSITE
WWW.RANDYBOOKS.NET, AMAZON.COM, AND
BARNESANDNOBLES.COM.

DATING:
DO MEN AND WOMEN DO IT ANYMORE?

By Randy Wallace

FORWARD

What happened to the good old days when people courted? What happened to the days when people talked and got to know each other before a date? What happened to the days when people would meet and talk about something other than sex? What happened to the days when people would do a meet and greet not a meet and sleep? What happened to the good old days when you could meet a nice person at the grocery store, car wash, or bus stop? What happened to the days when if you were single, your family and friends would try to fix you up with someone? What happen to the days when your mother was always trying to fix you up with someone in her church? Do people practice the art of talking, conversation, and getting to know each other before a date anymore?

Unfortunately, those days are gone forever. Now what most people (not all) do these days is chat, text, then have sex with a person without first getting to know anything about them. In these days, some people (not all) meet and have sex with a person before learning their last name. There's nothing wrong with that if you are not looking for a serious or meaningful relationship. I wasn't back in the day. I did a lot of meet and sleep. I did it for over thirty years. Back in the day, I had sex with hundreds of women. I didn't know some of their first names, so I just called them baby. I didn't know the last names for the majority of the women I was with. I didn't know anything about them. But I was not looking to make any of those women my wife or woman. They were there just to have sex with.

Today, there is not enough challenge for me in the dating game. It's too easy to meet and have sex a woman. All I do today is text, chat, meet and sleep - it is just that easy. Sometimes, I miss the challenges of the good old days.

DATING BACK IN THE DAY

We didn't have chatting or texting back in the day. If a man wanted to meet a woman, he had to have a good rap or a strong conversation. He had to know how to approach her, introduce himself to her, and hold her interest if he wanted to get anywhere with her. Back in the day, women made men work for their attention and affection (not all women, but most). Back in the day, when two people met and felt an attraction for each other, they would exchange numbers and talk by phone for a few days. If both felt comfortable with each other, then they would set up a date or a meet and greet. Now all people have to do is chat or text and it's on. This works with some people, not all.

I'm a retired player now and I wish we had chatting and texting back in the day. It would have made it much easier to get and sleep with a woman. The reason I say this is now that my player days are behind me, I'm looking for that special lady to have in my life. I'm finding it hard to find that special lady because it's too easy for a retired player to get sex texting and online chatting. All I have to do is chat or text to have sex with some women (not all women). There's no need for conversation anymore. There is no challenge in it for me.

Today, you can learn just about everything you wanted to know about a person just by texting and chatting. Now when couples meet and greet, there is nothing more to talk about but sex. The majority of the time, you have texted them all they need to know about you and they have texted you everything you need to know about themselves. Most people text you everything you need to know about themselves. This is usually done in a day or two after you two start texting. During texting and chatting, I am finding out that most people will tell you their life story. I am not a big fan of texting, but I do know it serves its purpose. I wonder and ask this question, do people feel more comfortable texting and chatting than they do face to face and talking? If you text a person all they need to know about you, when you do finally meet them, what do you talk about?

COMMUNICATION AND DATING

Communication is the most important thing you can have with that special person or any person. Communication will make a good marriage or relationship much better. The lack or absence of communication will bring a relationship to an end overnight. Ladies, thank about this: back in the day, if a man wanted to talk to a woman, he had to talk to her face to face. He had to know how to talk to her and know how to communicate with her. Now all he has to do is type a few words and it's all good with most women (not all women). He doesn't have to put in work with some women and try to get to know them. He doesn't even have to try to impress them. All he has to do is text, hyd, wyd, hru, ttyl, lol, lmbo, gm, and gn. This is how we communicate with each other most of the time. There is no face to face conversation or communication. We ask why our marriages and relationships don't work out. It's because we no longer communicate with each other anymore - all we do is text.

MY THREE CALL RULES

Online dating is the big thing now. Most people don't have the time to put in or time to try to meet that special person. It is so much easier to fill out a profile online and let that person come to you. Now that you have connected with someone and you two have been chatting back and forth for a few days, you feel comfortable enough with this person to exchange numbers. It's time to talk by phone. This is my three call rule. I will only call a person three times. If I do not get a response or reply by the third try, I will move on. Here's why:

1) I will call and leave a voice message with my name and my number and what site we chatted on. Normally a good time is after work when most people have settled in for the evening. I'll call one day and skip a day just to give that person a chance to reach out to me.
2) I will not call and hang up after the phone has rang a few times. I will wait to hear the voice recorder, then leave my message. When we exchange numbers, chatting and texting is over. We exchange numbers to talk.
3) I will no longer communicate with you by texting.

PHONE ETIQUETTE

What's up with phone communication? Do people even know how to leave a voice message when they call you and get your voicemail? I know some of you are saying, "I don't like to leave a message." Well how would a person know that you called? Are you that person that calls, lets the phone ring one time, and hang up just so your number will show up on their phone and you can say, "I called you?" People, if this has happened to you, leave those people alone. Block their number. If a person is interested in you, then they would want you to see and relay their message to you. Communication is very important when you are trying to start a new relationship. If a person is not able to communicate a voice message to you by voice mail, then how can they communicate with you in person? Oh! I forgot, texting is good enough for you.

TEXTING SHOULD NOT BE YOUR ONLY WAY TO COMMUNICATE

This is where a lot of people make their mistake. They exchange numbers and then allow a person to only communicate with you by texting. If a person can't talk on the phone after work but they can text all that day and evening, please move on. That person is not being honest about their status. A single person should able to take a phone call or make one anytime they like. I don't know how many times women have told me they text a guy and he will not return their text until three or four hours later. Or he will text them all day at work, but he will not return texts when he gets off work or when he is at home. Ladies, the reason for this is he can't. He has someone living with him and he can only text you if she is not there or he is alone in another room. Please move on. Don't waste your valuable time trying to find out why he is not texting you back. The answer is: he can't. He is not alone. Or if he will only text you during certain times of the day, please move on. Don't waste your time. Can you read the message he is sending you? He is involved with another woman and can only text you when she is not around. Move on. After you exchange numbers, then the texting needs to stop and the phone conversations need to start. If you two agree on a time to talk, call, don't text. That part is over. You text to meet, then now it's time to take the next step - talk and set up a meet and greet.

SPELLING AND SPELL CHECK

People, please review your spelling before you send it. Your spelling says a lot about you and your level of intelligence. Please review your message for spelling error. Before you send it, make sure you have properly spelled every word. I know these days when you are texting, we something cut our words short. If you are on an adult website, then you should chat and spell like an adult. If you are texting and you are an adult, then you should text and spell like an adult.

LADIES, DO YOU REMEMBER?

Ladies, remember back in the day when you and your man expressed your feelings for each other through touch and communication? Do you remember laughing and talking for hours? Do you remember how you loved to hear his voice when he would whisper in your ear? How you would sit and talk and watch TV together for hours? How you would laugh when he told you a joke? How it made you feel when he looked in your eyes and told you he loved you? Now all you get is a text from him. Is this how you choose to let him communicate his feelings to you? Ladies, do you prefer to read what he has to say to you or hear it come out of his mouth?

WHAT ARE YOU LOOKING FOR?

I have been asked this question by every woman I have met. My answer is always the same. I am not going to tell you what I am looking for in a woman. If I see something I like in you, I will tell you. The reason for this is I want you to be you and not what I am looking for. I don't want you to change from who you are to be who I want you to be. Think about this: how many times you have asked a person that question and they were honest with their answer? Or they told you they were looking for one thing and it turned out they were looking for something else? People will tell you what they think you want to hear just to get with you. Instead of asking a person what they are looking for, why don't you show them what they are missing out on by not being with you? If you are only looking for certain qualities or specific qualities in a person, then you may miss out on some qualities that person has that might be right for you. Everybody has their preference when it comes to the kind a person you want to date. That is a good thing, but not all people will measure up to your standards. Let's face the fact: the dating pool is not as full of good, eligible people to date these days. I am in no way telling to lower your standards, but you might have to adjust them a little bit.

LADIES, WHAT ARE YOU LOOKING FOR IN A MAN?

How many times has a man asked you this question on a date or online dating site? Was he happy with the answer you gave him? Ladies, what are you looking for in a man?
He has to be tall and handsome.
He has to a have a good job or a career.
He has to have money.
He has to have his own place and car.
He has to be good in the bedroom.

Ladies, these are just a few things I heard some of you say you are looking for in a man. There's nothing wrong with this. Every woman's needs and desires are different. Let me ask you a question: if a man has all of these things working for him, what would he need with just one woman when he could have one hundred women like I did? Back in the day, I had all these things working for me. I used them to meet and have sex with as many women as I could.

Ladies, remember this: a good man likes a good woman. They come in all shapes, sizes, colors, and work all types of jobs. He might have a heart as big as Texas and his love for you may be endless, but you will miss out because he doesn't meet your five qualifications.

Ladies, ask yourself, are you looking for a good man to have in your life or a man that has good things in his life? Stop choosing your man based on the things he has, the way he looks, or what he is like in bed. If that's all you want out of a man, then there are lots of men out there for you. If you are looking for something deeper than that, then you must look deeper. Stop being fooled by how he looks on the outside and look deeper into what is inside of him. Stop choosing a man based on want he has or what he can do for you. Then realize you have been doing all those thing by yourself. Remember this, ladies: if a man truly loves you, you will never have to tell him what you need him to do for you. He will already know what needs to be done.

WHAT ARE YOU LOOKING FOR IN A WOMAN?

Guys, how many times has a woman asked you this on a date or on an online dating site? Was she happy with the answer you gave her? Guys, ask yourselves this same question: What am I looking for in a woman?
She has to be slim with a pretty face, small waist, large breasts, and have a big, round booty.
She has to have a good job or career.

She has to have her own home and car.
She has to have her own money.
She has to be able to cook and clean a house, be a freak in the bedroom, and let me have a threesome with her and her friend.

Guys, if this is what you want in a woman, then that's okay. But ask yourself: if a woman has all these things working for her, why would she want one man when she can get as many men as she wants? Guys, a good woman likes a good man. They come in all shapes, sizes, colors, and work on all types of jobs. A good woman, just like a good man, is looking for someone that will respect her, love her, and will be there for her. Guys, in all my thirty plus years as a player, I have never met a bad woman. I have met a lot of women that have gone bad. Every time, it was because of something a man had done to her. Guys, remember these words: a happy wife can make you a happy life. Your happiness depends on how happy you make your wife.

IF IT WORKS, DON'T CHANGE IT

Ladies, let me share something with you. I hear you say all the time how you are tired of guys only talking about sex and asking for it before they get to know your name. You tell me this happens a lot online and in person. If a man is able to hold a conversation, with you it's usually all about sex. The reason for this is we men know if something works, you keep using it, no matter how dumb or stupid it might sound. Guys know that what he says to one woman might offend her, but another woman might find it flattening and a turn on. Men think like this: if he talks about sex to twenty women and only one responds and talks back to him, that's a win for him. Forget about the nineteen that blocked him or turned him down. Even though that old tired line he is trying to use on you didn't work, he will keep using it because it is still reliable and works on some women. Ladies, these guys are talking and saying these things because they are working on more women than you think. The words guys say to you might sound offensive and disrespectful to you, but they might be turning another woman on. We as men know if we talk dirty online to 20 women, we might offend 15 and get blocked by 4, but that 1 makes it all worthwhile. So if a man says something to you and you find it disrespectful or it offends you, don't let it get next to you. All that means is you are one of the 19 out of 20 women his words didn't work on.

ONLINE DATING

More talk about online dating. This is the most popular way to meet people these days. There are thousands of dating sites out there you can use to help find that special person for you. Instagram is another site you can use to meet people, but the most popular site is Facebook. These sites can be a good way to meet people, but you must still trust your own instincts about a person. A person can be whomever he/she wants to be online and you would never know who they truly are. Most people that use dating sites are honest about trying to find a friend that special someone. But unfortunately, there are people that use these sites for something else. These people will lie to you, deceive you, and try to scam you out of your money.

Ladies, let me say this to most of you who are on a free or low-cost dating website: why do you expect every man on there to be a gentleman? Please stop fooling yourselves. You get what you pay for. I know you say you have a friend or you know someone that met and maybe married a man or woman from the dating site, and yes, it does happen. And yes, people do win the lotto. But look at how many losers you have compared to the winners. Ladies, if you are seriously trying to find Mr. Right, then step your game up and subscribe to a website that has a good screening process. Yes, it might cost a little more money, but you won't meet Mr. Disrespectful on there. He does not want to go through the screening process and is damn sure not going to pay the extra money for being on it.

THE TOP FIVE DUMBEST THINGS TO ASK A PERSON ON AN ONLINE DATING SITE:

Tell me something about yourself.
Why are you on this site?
What are you looking for?
What do you like to do for fun?
Are you single?

People, if you would take the time to read a person's profile, you will find the answers to some if not all of these questions. If a person doesn't have them listed, then they are not serious about trying to find someone. A profile is used to tell you a little something about the person. It can be false, misleading, and misrepresenting. So use your own judgment and try to get to know the person outside of their profile.

PROFILE

A profile should only give out general information about you like your interests, hobbies, favorite sport team, favorite movie, or TV program. You shouldn't tell where you like to go or give the location, what days you will be there, where you work, or what kind of work you do. This information should only be given out when you have learned more about that person and feel comfortable around them. Wait until you have established a connection with that person before you give out your personal information. Giving out too much information on your profile, in my opinion, is not good. Why would a person want to meet you and get to know you when they have read all about you on your profile? Most dating sites say the more information you give out, the better your chances are of meeting people. I personally believe that you can give out too much information too quickly.

Be honest about what you have written about yourself. Your profile should be short and to the point. How many times have you read a profile that's more than a paragraph long? Ladies, on average, most men don't read profiles. If he is on a free dating site, that average goes up to 90 percent. Why do you think that when you start chatting with a person, they asked you what do you like to do for fun? It's there in your profile. They didn't read it. You could have written that you were the Queen of England and they will ask you where you work or what you do for a living. Be honest and up front about what you are looking for and have ZERO TOLERANCE for anything less.

LADIES, HERE ARE SOME TIPS THAT MIGHT HELP

Ladies, believe this: some men are just as shy or intimidated about online dating as you are. I know you might not believe this, but not only women have bad experiences with online dating. Men do too. Here are some tips and some things you need to stop saying to a man when you are chatting online:

"Blessed," "I'm blessed and highly favored," or, "Be blessed." Ladies what do you mean by saying these things? And what do they mean? Using these words to describe how you are doing or how your day is going does not give a man a way to come back to you with a response. Here's why: if a guy asks you how your day going and you say, "I'm blessed and highly favored," does that mean you are having a good day? Does it mean you are in good health? Does it mean you have no personal problems? Did you just get a raise or promotion at your job?

If you write, "Be blessed," after a sentence, does that mean you are done talking? The conversation is over and you're logging off? By saying these things, he doesn't know how to reply. Does he say anything or just log off? There is nothing wrong with the words, "I'm blessed." But if you are online chatting to the person on the other end, already know you are blessed to be alive. So if a guy asks you how are you doing or how your day is, say something like, "My day is great, thank you. How was yours." Or, "I'm great, thank you. How are you doing today?" By saying these words, you give him a way to come back to you and keep the conversation going.

Now, when you are ready to end the conversation, say something like, "I have to leave now. Can we chat later?" Please be polite. You don't have to be all "holy." Your profile says you attend church.

I'm looking for a God-fearing man or a church-going man.

Ladies, I was a player for 35 years. I was brought up in the church. My mom was a Sunday school teacher. She was over the BTU, Baptist Training Union. She taught Bible Study and I went to church at least twice every week. We went to Sunday School with her, morning services, and 3:00 p.m. programs. I can quote scriptures and say Bible verses. I know the Bible from Genesis to Revelation. I know church protocol and I am a God-fearing man and a player. I used all of these things to get women in the church and it was very easy.

Yes, ladies, players do believe in God, are God-fearing, and do go to church. I did. I had more women in church than out. Ladies, there are murderers, killers, child molesters, and women beaters that go to church. Bad men go to church just like good men and they all fear God. If a guy attends church with you a couple of times and can quote a scripture or two, does that mean you will date him and have sex with him? If you base your decision to date or have sex with a man only on the basis that he is God-fearing or he goes to church, then what does that say about you as a so-called God-fearing and church-going woman? Every man I know will give up a half day on Sunday of watching football to go to church with you if that's all he has to do to have sex with you.

Ladies, be tough and stay out of your damn feelings.

Ladies, stop taking everything these damn, fool ass men say to you so personally and seriously. Stop letting everything these fools, crazies, perverts, scammers, and needy ass men say to you get next to you. Don't let them upset you to the point where you think that all a man wants from you is sex, money, and a place to live. You should know most men have all these things. They are not trying to get them from you. There are females online trying to get the same things from men.

I get several hard luck stories every Thursday evening from women telling me their lights are about to get cut off. They need money to pay a light bill that is about to get cut off. They need money for gas for their car to take their child to the doctor. Their money hasn't made it on her EBT card and the kids don't have anything to eat. This is their birthday weekend and they don't have any money to go out and have a good time. Can I give them some money to celebrate? Ladies, this is what I say to them. Friday the only day the electric company cut off lights? Is Friday the only day you can take your kids to the pediatricians or doctor? Does the government forget to put money on people EBT cards every Friday of every month? Does a woman's car only run out of gas on Fridays? Ladies, how many birthdays do you have in a year? Men have to put up with the same perverts, scammers, fools, crazies, stalkers, and needy ass females just like you. Don't let them upset you. Do like I did. Take all those bad experiences and information and write a book. Maybe it would help someone. So enjoy the Internet dating site. Have fun on these sites and stop taking this damn mess so personally!

FEATURES ON A DATING SITE: DELETE AND BLOCK

Ladies, these features can be found on most dating sites. Use these buttons as often as you need. That is what it's for - to keep those crazies out of your life and off of your page.

LET'S TALK ABOUT STATUS

Status, in my opinion, is the most important pieces of information a person can put on a profile. This information will let you know if it's worth your time to chat with another person or not based on if they are available for dating. Now this information can be misleading, so please use your better judgment and follow your female instinct,

SINGLE

Single means a person who is not in any type of relationship and is looking for someone who is also single. If a person's profile says anything other than single, move on. Don't waste your time.

SEPARATED

This mean that two people are not together, but they haven't gotten a divorce. I don't understand. Why would you leave a person and take months or years to make it legal? You left them because you were not happy or they did something wrong to you. But you still have an attachment to them for some reason. People, if a person is separated and wants out of the marriage, they will make it happen legally as soon as possible. If not, they will be content with being separated for months or years. Please separate yourself from that person because they can't separate themselves from another person legally for some reason. People will start a new relationship with a new person before they have finished the old relationship with their spouse or the other person. People start new relationships before they finish the old one sometimes just to fill that void in their lives. Please use your better judgment with this separated person. Remember, they are still legally married - they just don't live together.

LEGALLY SEPARATED

This is something else I don't understand. Legally separated means that two people have a document that states they are legally separated but are still married by law. My question is why would you pay money to get a document stating that you are no longer together when you are still married? People spend money to get legally separated but not legally divorced. I don't understand that. If someone's profile says that they are legally separated, tell them to hit you back when their divorce becomes final. This legal separation may last months or years. Move on... don't waste your time.

IT'S COMPLICATED

If you see this on a person's profile, delete them or block them immediately. Nothing good will come from this. How is it complicated? You are either single, married, or in a relationship. What else is there? People say, "I'm in a marriage or in a relationship and things are not working out. But I'm not able to leave." I say that things are not working out because they are trying to get involved with someone else and not trying to work out their problems with the person they are with. If people would put as much time into trying to fix their marriage or relationship as they do trying find a new person on a dating site, it just might uncomplicated things. Please stay away from this person. Don't let their complication complicate your life.

DIVORCED OR WIDOWED

This means that two people are no longer married and they have the proper paper work to prove it. I'm not saying what a person's status says on their profile makes them a bad person, but sites put this information there for a reason. It is so you will at least know a little something about the person you are chatting with. Not all people will be honest and truthful about their status and their intentions, but trust your feelings and instincts. They have never led you wrong before.

PHOTOS AND PICTURES

Please be honest, men and women. Be honest about the pictures you post online. Make sure your pictures are current and up-to-date. Let a person like you for who you are, not for the person you are trying to be.

Ladies, please stop posting pictures of yourself from when you were in high school. I have seen the prom queen picture, the high school cheerleader picture, and those old glamour shot pictures you took ten, fifteen, or twenty, years ago when you were fine and sexy. Ladies, please stop misleading and misrepresenting yourselves online. A guy sees your picture and he think he's going to meet a hot, sexy, attractive lady. You show up looking like Aunt Ester from Sanford and Son or Celia from The Color Purple or Precious from the movie. You show up with a big belly, wide butt, and sagging breasts - shame on you. Ladies, post pictures of you and only you. Not you and your family, not you and your kids, not you and your friends, not you and your co-worker. You are trying to find someone for you not them. Stop posting pictures of your nail, your toes, your hair, and your tattoos. You may think that makes you look good, but it makes you look hood and ghetto. Ladies, let me share something with you: when most men see these pictures, they think you are desperate, needy, and starving for attention.

Guys, stop misrepresenting yourselves. Stop posting old pictures of you ten to twenty years ago, when you had a six-pack stomach, played high school football, and were tall, dark, and handsome. Guys, ladies see these pictures and think she is meeting this fine guy with a nice body, six-pack abs, and good looks. You show up looking like Mr. Brown from the TV show Meet the Browns or Pops from the movie Friday. You had six-pack abs. Now you are suffering from DD (Dunlap Disorder). Your belly done lap over your waist band. You have a bad odor coming from your body. You have three or four teeth in the front of you mouth. Your breath smells like you been eating fish (ladies, you know what I mean). Guys, stop posting pictures of you and your car, you and your money, and your body parts. Guys, you are trying to meet her, not run her off.

People, please stop deceiving and misleading each other about who you are and what you looking like. If you don't love yourself and how you look, then how do you expect anyone else to love you? Beauty is in the eyes of the beholder. Remember, for every picture you like on a dating website, hundreds of people might like it too. Never think you are the only one that a person is chatting with or that you are the only one who likes that picture.

SELFIES

People, there is nothing wrong with taking selfies of yourself in your home or when you are out on the town. But please make sure your damn house is clean when you take a selfie at your home. How many times have you seen selfies of people in their homes and there are kid's toys all over the floor, clothes on the sofa, or trash on the floor? You post this picture online for millions of people to see how nasty you are, with beer cans and empty liquor bottles on the coffee table. You are taking a selfie with all this in the background and you think you look good, but people are laughing at you and how junky your house is.

People, why are you taking selfies of yourself in your damn bathroom? The bathrooms are a private place for you to be alone, but you take pictures of yourself there. You are in the mirror of the bathroom in your home, talking a selfie. On the countertop of the sink is deodorant, tooth paste, mouthwash, hair weave, a curling iron, a blow dryer, styling gel, make-up and even your female personal products. These items are all cluttered on your bathroom counter top. You are talking a selfie with all those things showing. You take a selfie of yourself and your nasty shower curtain showing in the background with 3-4 dirty towels hanging over it. You think you look cute, but you don't. You look nasty. Some of you take pictures of yourself when you are out at the club or in a restaurant. You just have to take a selfie when you are in the restroom. You don't care if you are by the toilet, the sink, or the urinal. You don't care! You will take a selfie. Then you post it for millions of people to see you smiling with a toilet bowl in the background. You are sick!

SELFIES OF FOOD

People, please eat your damn food and stop taking pictures of it. Everybody knows what chicken wings, pizza, shrimp, fish, and hamburgers looks like. You go out to a restaurant and order food. Before you eat it, you have to take a damn picture of it to remind yourself of what you ate a couple of hours ago. Are you take pictures of the food that someone else has brought you because you were too cheap to buy it or couldn't afford to pay if it yourself? If so, why do you post it for everyone to see? When you are done cooking food at your home, before you serve it, you take a selfie of you and the food. Most of the time when people see it, they say they wouldn't even feed that food to their dog. People, just because your food looks good does not mean it tastes good. Remember, the apple looked good to Eve. You know how that turned out.

A LITTLE IS A LOT

People, you don't need twenty or thirty pictures of yourself on your profile. It makes you look desperate. Two or three nice body shots are good. Think about it: when you see a person with a lot of pictures, most of the time, they are wearing the same outfit. Or they just moved their head or body left or right. Ladies, some of you, not all, are posting these provocative photos. You are half naked, your breasts are all out, your butt is up in the air, you are looking at your butt, you are bent over with your legs open, and you say you are not looking for sex. What the hell are you looking for? To a man, you are advertising sex. That's why you are being talked to the way you are - because you are sending a message that you are easy. Remember, the picture you post says a lot about the lady you are. If you post provocative and sleazy pictures, you are going to attract sleazy men.

Ladies, I hear you say, "My pictures are not like that and I still attract those men." There are thousands and thousands of men online looking at your profile. Yes, you are going to get some crazies and perverts from time to time. I say that comes with the site, but you may lessen your chance of these men contacting you if you are not advertising sleazy sexual pictures on your page. Remember ladies, what you put on the web is out there forever. Just because you delete your profile, it sometimes remains on that site. Just because you delete your profile, it does not mean that someone somewhere doesn't have a picture of you with your ass up in the air or you bent over showing your ass. One day, you might see these pictures again. Even worse, your child or grandchildren might see them. What are you going say if five, ten, fifteen, or twenty years later, they come to you and say, "Mom or Granny, why does my friend have a picture of you showing your ass.?"

NO PICTURE, HEAD SHOTS ONLY, CARTOON MAGAZINES, OR WORDS: NO!

The above mentioned are red flags. If a person is serious about trying to find someone, they would go all out to show that they are a good catch. They will try to give themselves the most exposure possible.

Head shot only: I would be very careful chatting with someone with only a head shot photo. They might be hiding that body for a reason. How many of you took a chance on a head shot only picture, and when you met that person, that body was jacked up or a hot mess? When you finally met that person, you wish you had deleted them from the start.

Cartoon magazine photos: I thank these people are crazy. Why would you post a picture of a cartoon character or one from a magazine ad if you or trying to meet someone? I have a full body picture of me on my site. Why can't you post one of yourself on your site? Who are you hiding from?

No photos or words: Do not accept this person. If they are truly interested and want to meet you, they would let you know what they look like. People say they will post one later. I would say, "When you do, then you hit me up. You can see me; why can't I see you?"

TIME STAMP PHOTO

I think this is the best way to ensure that the person you are chatting with looks like themselves. This is not 100% accurate, but I think it gives you the best opportunity that the person you are looking at in the photo will look the same in person.

NEVER POST PICTURES OF YOUR CHILD OR CHILDREN

People, PLEASE stop putting pictures of your child or children and grandchildren on these adult dating sites. NEVER post a picture of a child on an adult website. Adult dating sites are for adults only. NEVER put a child's picture on one. You never know who is looking at that child. They could be child molesters, pedophiles, child sex offenders, or the devil himself. They all use these dating sites too, and you are advertising your child to them. Only adult pictures should be posted on an adult website or dating site. I know they are cute, but please don't put their pictures on an adult site. You never know who is looking at your babies and what they are thinking about doing to them. You might think a person is interested in you, and all the time they want your child. PLEASE keep your babies safe and off these adult dating sites.

CATFISHING AND LONG-TERM DATING

Remember, there are a lot of people online that are not being truthful about who they are or what they are looking for. If you meet person and you chat and feel comfortable enough with them, then it is time to meet them. If a person keeps coming up with excuses for why they can't meet you, chances are, they are hiding something from you. Don't spend weeks, months, or years chatting with a person only to find out they are not who they say they are.

NEVER GIVE OUT YOUR EMAIL ADDRESS

I say this because if a person contacts you on a dating site and wants to chat, then why would you need to chat with them by email? They did not contact you by email. Why do they want to chat with you by email? These people might be up to something. Just say no! We can chat on the site or we won't chat at all - or just move on.

MEET AND GREET IS NOT A DATE

Remember, a "meet and greet" is not a date. This is a way to meet a person and get a first look at them to see what they look like and let them see what you look like. You can make a decision if there is going to be a first date. A meet and greet should be kept short. Meet somewhere for coffee, ice cream, or a soda. Meet Starbucks or a coffee house so you can get a beverage that doesn't take long to finish. If you have a meet and greet with someone and they have misrepresented themselves with their photo, you don't have to sit there for an hour mad, looking at them as they eat their food. This does not mean that you are cheap, but we have all been misled before. If your meet and greet goes well, make it last a little longer. A meet and greet can last as long as it takes for you to drink your coffee or soda. A good meet and greet can last five minutes or five hours, which can make a good first date even better.

MY MEET AND GREET STORIES

Meet and Greet Story #1:

I met a lady online. We chatted for a couple of weeks. Eventually, we decided to do a meet and greet at Starbucks at 2:00 p.m. I got there at 1:45 p.m. and waited until 2:15 p.m. I got a call from her telling me she had run out of gas on the highway. She said she let her son use her car to go to the club the night before and he didn't put any gas in it. Now she is out of gas on the freeway. She didn't have any money for gas and asked if I could come and get her, bring her some gas, or bring money for gas.

"Did you call your son?" I asked her.

"I did," she said, "But he is too busy and can't come get her."

"You let him use your car and he ran all the gas out, I said. "Now you are stranded on the highway and he is too busy to come and help you? Look on the back of your driver's license. There is a number you can call for road side service. They will bring you gas." When I got home, I blocked her profile and that was that. I don't have time for games.

Meet and Greet story #2:

I had been chatting with this lady for a week of two. We set up a meet and greet at the park. She showed up on time and looked just like her profile. We talked about an hour and things were good. After talking, I walked her to her car. She turned and asked me if I could give her a hundred dollars. She said her check had not made it to her debit card and she needed to play her bills and buy food for her kids. I told her I was broke too. I didn't have any money. Then she asked me to give whatever I had to her, even ten to twenty dollars was okay. I told her I didn't have a dime. She got mad, got in her car, and burned off. I went home and blocked her. I don't have time for games.

These are just two of my many stories. I have lots more and I bet you do too. What I'm telling you is to have zero tolerance for scammers, games, con artists, and crazies. Don't put up with their mess and don't be bullied by anyone online. That's what the "DELETE" and "BLOCK" button is for. Use it and use it often.

DATING AND THE FIRST DATE

This is the most important stage of all. If you have reached this point, this means the meet and greet went well. Now you and that person seem to have some chemistry or something in common. It's time for the first date. People, let's be real about something: the economy has hit everybody's pockets. So let's be sensible and reasonable about where we go and what we eat. I suggest Chili's or Applebee's because they have a great two for $20 menu. TGI Fridays also has a great menu. They have some very good food at reasonable prices. You can get dinner and a couple of drinks for about thirty dollars.

ADVICE FOR THE LADIES

Ladies, please be on time. You only get one chance to make a first and lasting impression. Dress nice and appropriately. Let all your Facebook followers and your girlfriends know that you will be off your phone and the site for an hour. You are all dressed up and looking very nice. Make him focus all of his attention on you not your cell phone. Ladies, don't try to break the bank. Only order as much food as you can eat. Don't order food to take home for the next day or food to take home to your kids.

ADVICE FOR THE MEN

Guys, get your hygiene together. Please wash your body, brush your teeth, and shave. Wear clothes that fit and that are in style. Learn how to hold a conversation with proper and correct English. Be a gentleman at all times. Open the door on her side of the car, open the door for her when you enter the restaurant, let your lady enter the restaurant before you, and let her be seated before you. Turn off you phone. Let your boys, Facebook followers, and baby mamas know you will be out of pocket for an hour. Guys, please, please have the money to pay for the meals. If you don't have at least $50, then don't try to take a lady out to dinner. Even though you took her to a two for $20 dinner, she might want dessert or a drink.

LADIES, DATING TIPS THAT WILL KEEP YOU SAFE

Ladies, get a pre-paid phone card and use it for your point of contact. If it doesn't work out between you and him, you don't have to worry about him calling you or texting. You can block him on your cell, but he can still text you.

Make the first date for the day time. It's safer that way. Here's why: if you meet a guy at night and the date didn't turn out the way he wanted it, you don't know what this guy will do. When you leave the restaurant at night, you can't see him. He just might be following you home and you wouldn't even know it because it's dark. The first date should always in the day time, never at night. Remember, you know nothing about this man.

Always put gas in your car in the day time before a date or after work. Never stop to get gas at night after a date or leaving the club. It is not safe.

Never go to his place or let him come to yours for the first date.

Arrive at the meeting place a few minutes early and try to get a parking spot close to the front entrance so you can see him pull up before he sees you. This way you can see if he looks like his picture he posted.

Don't order the most expensive thing on the menu or go to the most expensive restaurant.

Ladies, please dress appropriately. This might be Mr. Right. Remember, the first impression of you will be the one he will always remember.

Stop taking pictures of the damn food. Can you just tell everybody on Facebook what you had for dinner?

Don't talk or listen to stories about his past relationships. If he is truly over her and has truly moved on, then there is nothing to talk about.

Talk to him to try to find out if you have anything in common or if you have some of the same interests. You can learn a lot about a person from a good conversation.

I hope these tips help you to meet that right man and maybe take it to the next level. Have fun with dating. It's a great way to meet new people. Remember, dating is just a way to gather information and learn about a person. There is no sex in dating and both people are free to date as many people as they like.

MY DATING STORY

I met this lady online. We chatted for about a week and then we set up a meet and greet at a Starbucks for coffee. It went well, so we made plans for our first date. I asked her where she would like to go or what she would like to do. "Dinner and drinks will be fine," she said.

"Okay," I said. "Where would you like to go?" She picked one of the nicer and more expensive restaurants in town. We set a time and a day to meet for dinner at 7 p.m. Friday night. I made it to the restaurant about 6:45 p.m. She called and said she was running late, but that she would be there in thirty minutes.

"Okay," I said. "I will go inside and have a drink." She arrived at 7:40 p.m. – remember, the date was for 7:00 p.m. We were seated for dinner. She kept getting text messages and responding to them. Then when we ordered our food. She orders a $30 meal.

"Are you sure you can eat all that food?" I asked her. She said yes. As we waited on our food, she was continuing to text on the phone. "Would you like to step outside to talk to that person and let them know you are at dinner?" I asked her.

"No," she said. "I'm done." Just then our food came. It looked so delicious that she took a picture of it. She then gave me her phone so I could take a picture of her and the food. As I was eating, I noticed she was hardly eating her food.

"Is everything alright?" I asked her. "Is there something wrong with the food?"

"No," she said. "I'm a slow eater." I am done eating at this point and ask for the check. She asks for a to-go-container for her food.

"This restaurant does not have to-go-containers," I told her. "I thought you knew that. Haven't you eaten here before? You chose this restaurant."

"No," she said, "I only heard about it from my friends." As the waiter came with the check, she asked for a to-go-container.

"I am sorry, miss," he said, "We don't have them here."

"What about all this food?" she asked.

"It's going into the trash," I told her. As we were walking out of the restaurant, I saw her looking back at all that good food she was not going to get to take home and eat later. That was my first and last date with her.

DATING AND COURTING: DO MEN AND WOMEN DO IT ANYMORE?

Dating and counting: do men and women do it anymore. Back in the day, men and women would gather information to see if they were interested in one another. That was it! There was no sex in dating and courting. Some of you now think that if you have sex with a person or have been on a few dates with this person, it means you are in a relationship with that person. No! Ladies, I see you make this mistake all the time. Dating a man and having sex with him before you get a commitment from him does not mean you are in a relationship with him. Ladies, men don't see it like you do. If a man can have sex with you without being committed to you, that is a win for him. He will continue to have sex with you as long as you give it to him. Ladies, if you haven't talked to him about a personal relationship or do not have a commitment from him to you, it just free sex. If you haven't set any ground rules or established an understanding with that man about the kind of relationship you are looking for, then you are just having sex with him. What makes you think you and that man are in a committed relationship if he hasn't committed to you? Do you think that if you date a guy for a few days or weeks and then you start having sex with him, that you and that man are now automatically in a relationship? No! Men do not see it that way. Sex without a commitment, to a man, is just free sex.

Men, if you spend your hard-earned money on a lady, buying her nice things, taking her out to dinner, to the movies, pay a bill, or get her nails and hair done, does that mean she is your woman? No! Do you think that means you and her are in a relationship? No! In a court of law, that's called a gift to her. Guys, before you spend your money, get an understanding of where you stand with her. Ladies, before you have sex with a man, make sure he understands that you two are in a committed relationship. Men see dating as something he must do just to have sex with you. You make it easy by having sex with him without any commitment from him.

COURTING

Ladies, take notes from your grandmothers and great-grandmothers. Ask them how a man should court a woman. How should a woman act when been courted? What should you expect from a man? Stop moving too fast, slow down, and allow a man to court and date you. Demand this from him. If you know your self-worth, then demand to be treated like a lady with the respect you deserve. Please stop thinking that just because you gave a man your body, that you and he are in a relationship. That is not how he sees it. Stop fooling yourself thinking that having sex with a man makes you a couple or exclusive. He doesn't see it that way.

COURTING BACK IN THE DAY

Back in your grandparent's day, if a young man wanted to talk, date, or court a man's daughter, he would first ask permission from her father. If her father approved, then he would ask the young man questions. Who are you and where are you from? Who are your folks? Do you have a job? What kind of work do you do? What church do you attend and who is your pastor? What are your intentions with my daughter? Yes, fathers back in the day did ask these questions and many more. If the answers the young man gave him didn't meet his satisfaction or approval, then there was no talking or courting. The father did these things to see if the young man was even worthy of talking to or courting his daughter and to see if he would be able to take care of her. Now a chat or a text from a guy is all it takes to get some of you in bed. I wish your grandpa could see just how easy it is now for a man to get his granddaughter. Now all a man has to do to have sex with some women is just send a text.

LADIES, DEMAND THAT YOU BE DATED OR COURTED

Your grandmother and great-grandmother knew how a man should court or date a woman, how a woman should be treated, and that she shouldn't accept anything less from a man. They knew how men should treat a woman, how a woman should act, and what she should do during the courting process. Ladies, stop being so quick to meet and sleep with a man. I hear you ladies say a man doesn't know how to date a woman or court a woman anymore. Ladies, it's your fault because you have stopped demanding to be courted and dated. Like I said at the start of this book, you have to make a man work for what he wants. Aren't you worth it?

STOP BEING HIS ROUTINE, A NORMAL NANCY

A man knows that most women, not all, will settle for the same thing from every man. This is what you usually do on a date. Dinner, a movie, walk in the park, drinks, clubbing, plays, concert and/or bowling. That's not a date. That's a damn routine. You do the same things and go to the same places with every new guy you meet. A man knows he doesn't have to work for your affection, just take you out on the weekend for dinner, drinks, and a movie. He knows if it works on one woman out of twenty, that's a win for a man - and you are being that one. He knows if he does one or two of these things with you, it will get him whatever he wants. He knows you are that easy. He knows doing these things will get him sex with most women, not all, and he is cool with that.

CHALLENGE HIM TO BE CREATIVE

Ladies, challenge that man to be more creative about dating. You have him. Think of new places he can take you. Back in my player days, when I was trying to date a woman, I would ask her to write down five of her favorite things she liked doing. Then I would take that list, read it, and come up with five different things she has never done before. Get him out of is comfort zone. Make him think outside of his box. I'm not saying challenge his manhood or be aggressive toward him, but challenge him to come up with new places to go, new sights to see, new things to do, new foods to eat. Ladies, you should stop being a Normal Nancy. Stop letting him take you to the normal places. He takes all his other dates to the movies, dinner, drinks, plays, concerts, and bowling. These are not dates, this is a habit, a routine. Now you are part of it. Just like when he gets up in the morning and put his shirt, shoes, and pants on - its all part of his routine.

Ladies, are these places the only places you like to go for entrainment and fun? Challenge yourself to come up with new ways to spend a day or evening. A date shouldn't always be about finances, the best restaurants, hottest night spots, or the newest vineyards. Think about this: your grandparents didn't have a lot of money or a lot of nice places to go when they were courting. But they still managed find ways to entertain each other and have fun - all without having sex or spending a lot of money. A friendly courtship makes a good friendship that leads to a great relationship that turns into lifelong marriage. Some of them last for 30, 40, 50, or 60 years. They all started out by courting, dating, talking, and just getting to know each other.

DATING CAN TAKE PLACE DAY OR NIGHT AND THROUGH THE WEEK

Most people think a date can only happen at night for dinner, drinks, and a movie or on the weekend. That's what I call routine dating and that's the way a lot of people date. I feel so sorry for you because you are missing out on so much by being a routine weekend dater. There are lots of ways and things to do during the week. Stop being that weekend routine dater. I know we all work during the week and you are tired when you get off. Or you may not have the money during the week to go out on a date. You don't need to leave your home to have a date. There are lots of thing you can do during the week. I call them weekly dating. Here are a few things you can do during the week with your date.

Grill outside and have dinner on the patio or back porch.

Do a movie night. Invite your date over to watch TV or a movie.

Get together and prepare a dinner for two for the evening.

Talk over drinks and get to know each other.

Get together for a game night. Play board games cards or dominoes.

These are just five things you and your date can do during the week. You don't have to wait until the weekend to have a date. Be creative! Find new things to do during the week and you will have lot more time to do something for yourself on the weekend. Please stop this weekend routine dating.

Date and Cook at Home

Dating can get expensive. Going out to dinner and a movie can be costly. I say, why not date and have dinner at home? Why don't the two of you prepare a meal together and spend the evening talking, watching TV, or a movie? Here are ten meals you can prepare that cost under ten dollars:

1) Spaghetti with meat sauce, salad and garlic bread
2) Baked chicken with green beans and potatoes
3) Grilled pork chops, mac-and-cheese and spinach
4) Stir-fry with beef or chicken
5) Baked or grilled fish, shrimp, or salmon with a salad and garlic bread
6) Fried chicken with mashed potatoes and mixed vegetables
7) BLT with sliced turkey, ham, or chicken and potato chips
8) Taco, chicken, or beef salad
9) Fried fish, French fries, a salad, and garlic bread
10) Hamburger Helper of any kind.

You can fix that up to look like a gourmet meal. Who don't like Hamburger Helper? Just add two vegetables.

These are just ten dishes you can prepare together or have ready for your date. They don't take long to prepare and cost under ten dollars. Most of the ingredients, you might already have in your pantry or freezer. You can also find them at your local, corner dollar store. Last but not least, introduce wine with your meal. You don't have to spend money to have a good time dating - just be creative. I got a lot of compliments about my cooking skills back in my player days. Most women were surprised to see that a man could prepare a nice meal. This does not mean you are trying to be cheap, but this will replace that routine dating.

Let me explain that most people say they are too tired to do anything when they get off work. You are right about that. Most people, when they get off work, want to go home and relax, or have to go home and deal with the kids. They wait until the weekend to go out or on a date. This is where you are cheating yourself. Think about this: some people wait until Friday to go out or on a date, but the majority of people wait until Saturday because they are tired or have things to do Friday evening. The people that go out on Friday spend all day Saturday running errands and doing things they didn't have time to do during the week. Most of them are getting ready for Sunday morning church service, work, or something else.

The people that go out on Saturday spend Friday running errands so they won't have to do them Saturday or Sunday. They are at church, at home resting, and getting ready to go back to work Monday. Look at it this way: you work five days a week. The majority of you attend church service once or twice on Sundays. After that, you go out to dinner with family, prepare dinner at home, or just stay at home and relax. So you work five days week. Sundays is almost always busy, so you only have 4-6 hours a week, maybe on the weekend, to have a good time for yourself. If you don't believe me, sit down and look at your weekly routine. You don't have time for dating. That's why I say, go a short date during the week. Two to three hours will work depending on where you and that person are with each other... maybe make it a sleepover? This will free up more time for you on the weekend because you have given the person who you are dating what they want most from you - some of your time. This will help you break the routine dating cycle that the majority of you are in.

In my opinion, there are three reasons why people do not date during the week. There may be more, but I think these three can sum it up for most daters:

Only one person has his or her own place. This is where most of the dating takes place. This can be a problem because at times, the person with their own place is going to get tired of having the dates at their place all the time.

Distance: this is when the two people who are dating might stay in another city or town. It is just too far to drive there and back home. If this is the case, plan a sleep over. You might have to leave a little early the next day. Switch days so one person will not have to do the driving all the time.

Lack of time. Like I said earlier, people are busy during the week and time is something a lot of them don't have. It doesn't take a lot of time to sit down and have a meal. How long do you spend in a restaurant having dinner? An hour or an hour and a half is all you need to spend on dinner date at home. If you want to do other things, make it a short dinner so you are done eating in an hour or less. That will give you time to do something else you might want to do later. Let's say you get there at 7:00 p.m. Dinner starts and is over at 7:45 or 8 p.m. You have an hour to do whatever you want to do and will still make it home by 10:00 p.m. or sooner. Most people don't start getting ready for bed until then. The earlier the date starts, the sooner you will be back at home. So plan to do more dating during the week and have some of your weekend time to yourself.

DATING AT HOME DOES NOT HAVE TO ALWAYS BE ABOUT SEX

Dating at home does not have to always be about sex. It should be about two people spending quality time being together and enjoying each other. Back in my True Player days, my home was female friendly. A lady could come over and feel comfortable and safe being there. I had everything a woman needed - the ambiance and décor set the mood for the evening. I had everything from scented candles to her favorite, wine, cocktail, or beverage. The first thing a woman would do when she came into my home was to take off her shoes, sit on the sofa, and enjoy a drink while eating a bowl of fruits. She knew what was coming next: a foot massage or shoulder massage while she watched TV or a movie. My home had everything any woman needed: her favorite food, drink, shower gel, bubble bath, and female products. They were not out for every woman to see, but the things she needed, she had. Sometimes, it was not about sex. Sometimes, a woman just needs to be pampered to relieve some of the stress in her life. Some women would come over to my home and sit in a hot bubble bath, have a drink, listen to some good music, get out of the tub, get in the bed, and take a nap for an hour or so. Then they would get up and go home feeling good and refreshed. Like I said, it was not all about sex.

A True Player like I was back in the day knew that a woman needs more from a man than sex. That is what I gave her. One-on-one time is best spent getting to know and learn more about each other. As a True Player, I didn't try to have sex with every woman that came to my house, but I did try to learn all I could about her. When that time came, I would know what to do to please and satisfy her.

ARE YOU READY TO DATE?

I ask this question because I have seen many people trying to date when they need to be trying to get their life back together. Dating should be the last thing they should be trying to do. I have family members and friends that come out of marriages and relationships that they have been in for months or years. When it ends, they get right back in the dating game and bring their old feelings into a new relationship. You wonder why your new relationship doesn't work out. It's because you are not done with your last marriage or relationship. You are in two relationships and you don't even know it. You are still trying to figure what happened or what went wrong with your last relationship at the same time you are trying to start a new one. People, please hold off trying to date until you are emotionally, mentally and financially done with that marriage or relationship. Don't take that hurt, anger, bad feelings, and bad debt into a new relationship. Take as much time as you need to get your life together and get over that last relationship. Please don't hurt another person just because someone has hurt you.

ARE YOU FINANCIALLY ABLE TO DATE?

Due to the economy, a lot of people are finding themselves out of work or losing their jobs, homes, and cars. People, this is not the time to be trying to date. Your only focus should be trying to get your life back together - not trying to date or join an online dating site. How many times have you met a person online or in person and they don't have a job? How can you date without money? People, how many times have you met a person on a dating site or in person and they don't have their own place? They live with their mother, sibling, son, daughter, friends or a family member. Why are they are trying to date and don't even have a place to stay? Where are they going to take you after the date is over?

Car transportation: if you don't have this, how can you even get to your date? I am not downing anyone's situation, but people, you need all three of these things to successfully date: money, a car, and a place to live. Now there are some people out there that will date you with one, two, or none of these things. May God bless them, but I am not one of those people. Are you?

MEET MY MOM AND FAMILY

People, how many times have you met a person, dated for a few weeks, maybe a month - and he or she takes you home to meet their mom and family? When you met them, you are all excited. When you are introduced to them, you come away feeling like they don't like you and are not interested in trying to get to know you. This is because the person you are with has taken so many people over the years to meet mom and family that mom and the family wonders why they should get to know you when he or she will have someone new for them to meet at the next family gathering. People, stop taking everybody you meet to meet your mom and family.

Ask yourself, how many people have you taken to meet your mom and family in a year? If your answer is more than one person in a year, then you have what I call, "Chronic Meet My Mom and Family Disorder." This comes from when a person has to show off his or her date to mom and family just to get their approval. This is because the person you are dating has either been in two or three bad marriages or several bad relationships that didn't work out. This person is trying reassure themselves that you are better than the last person they brought to meet mom or the family. I personally think that mom and the family should be happy and excited to meet you. They need to feel that you have finally met the right person. Not that you have brought the right person for now, but you will have someone new at the next family gathering.

MEET MY CHILD OR CHILDREN

People, especially women, stop taking every man to meet your child or children. Ladies, I have seen this happen thousands of time.

Ladies, when you meet a man and you hit it off, you like him and he seems to like you. Everything is going right between you two. You have been dating for a couple of weeks - then you introduce that man to your child or children. Stop! Do not do that anymore. Stop and ask yourself: how many men have you introduced to your child or children in one year? If it's more than one, shame on you, mom. You should not expose your child or children to every man you meet. Ladies, I am not saying that all of you do this. But to the ones that do expose their child or children, please stop! People, please stop introducing every man you meet to your child or children.

People, how can we teach our children about commitment and relationships when they see us going through two, three, or four a year? We all try to teach our kids the right way to do things. Shouldn't that include teaching by example? We expect our kids to do what we say. How can they when you say one thing and do something different? Ladies, you teach your little girls that her body is a temple and it should not be given to every man. You tell her to wait and save herself for marriage or for that special man. Ladies, ask yourself, by the age of 18, how many men has your little girl seen you sharing your temple with? Ask yourself, how many times has she waken you up the next morning and you had a man in your house you hardly knew> Ask yourself, how many men she has gotten to know and like only to learn that you have broken up with him and now you have someone new you want to introduce to her? Ladies, I am by no means talking about all of you. But to the ones who can relate to what I am talking about, you know who you are. Please stop! You deserve better and your baby girl does too.

Guys, we teach our boys how to conquer but not care, how to lie but not love, how to cheat but not commit, how to hurt but not help, how to disrespect rather than respect. Guys, we are much worse than women. We will take every woman we date around our sons so they can see how it's done. We think the more women our sons see us with, the more successful he will be with women. We believe this is how a man is supposed to teach his son about women. The sad thing about it is that most men, not all, think they are doing the right thing by their sons. Guys, there is an old saying that goes like this: what you send out you will get back. So when your baby girl comes to you, crying, telling you about the man that hurt her and disrespected her, don't get upset. That man is only doing what his dad taught him, just like what you are teaching your son.

DATING SHOULD BE FUN

Dating should be fun! It should be a way to meet new people and maybe make a new friend. Enjoy dating. Please be careful and take all the time you need to find that special person just for you. Remember, there is no sex in dating. Both people are free to date as many people as they like. Dating is only a way to gather information about a person to help you make up your mind on if you want to take that next step. Good luck, have fun, and be safe. May God bless your new life with the person He has chosen for you.

LONG DISTANCE DATING: HOW FAR WILL YOU GO TO MEET A PERSON?

I have a 25-mile limit on how far I will go to meet a person. I am not a long distance dater. If long distance dating works for you, great. But how many times has it worked out? Long distance relationships can work, but they are very challenging and take more effort than a regular, in-town relationship. If you do long distance dating, here are some tips for you.

Always get a hotel close to the airport.

NEVER stay at the person's home.

Make the first visit a weekend visit or no more than 2-3 days.

Demand an updated picture of the person you are going to see. Leave it with a friend of family member.

Make sure, when you get to where you are going, you take a picture with the person. Add as much information about that person as you can, like color of car, where they are taking you, etc., and text the picture and message to a friend or family member.

Always have a backup plan just in case things don't work out. Try to find out as much as you can about the city you are going to.

Make frequent calls or texts to friends or family to let them know you are.

Have a code word you use when you text or call so they will know it is you.

Be aware of your surroundings at all times. If something does not feel right, then do not go there.

PEOPLE, JUST ENJOY IT

I said this earlier in this book, if you meet someone and you hit it off, and you are enjoying each other's company, don't mess it up by trying to label it. Don't mess it up by trying to name it, analyze it, or define it. People, how long has it been since you met someone and you have a good time together? You like them and they like you. You do things together, share things together, and they made you feel great being with them. Then you have to go mess everything up by asking these questions. Where is this going? Are we in a relationship? When are we going to take it to the next level? People, can you just enjoy the fact that you are happy for once? Can you just enjoy the good way this person makes you feel? Can you just enjoy finally having someone in your life that makes you smile or laugh? Can you just enjoy the fact that you have finally met a good person? Can you for just once in your life enjoy this experience with this good person without trying to marry or start a relationship with this person? Can you for once allow yourself to be happy without being in a marriage or relationship? People, not all dates will lead to a relationship. Not all relationships will lead to marriage. Do you not believe that sometimes people come into our lives because we deserve to be happy and have a good time? If by chance the things turn sexual, that's okay too.

Remember what I said about sex and dating, but that decision is up to you. When sex comes into play, things change. You are both grown adults. Just be honest about what you want and what you are looking for. If they agree to what you ask for, great. If not, that's good too. Let them move on. Remember, you don't have to be in a marriage or a relationship to have fun and enjoy life with another person.

WHEN IS IT TIME FOR SEX

I get asked this questions all the time. My answer is this: it's up to you and how you feel about a person. Sex happens because two people want it to happen. It can happen in one day, week, one month, or longer. It all depends on how two people feel about each other. People are all different and you feel a different way toward every new person you met. I say, be honest with yourself about what you want and how you feel about a person. It is my opinion that after you have been with a person for a while, you will make up your mind on whether you want to friend them or f**k them. We all are grown men and women and we know what we want.

The worst thing you can do is to fool yourself into thinking that if you are having sex with a person, that mean you are in a relationship with that person. If you have sex on the first day or in the first week, you feel like you are a bad person. If you wait weeks or months, that will make things seem better to you when you do have sex with that person because you feel you have waited long enough. I say, have sex whenever you feel like it, but PLEASE use PROTECTION and PROTECT yourself at all times. Remember this: you can get STD, HIV or AIDS if you have sex on the first date, the fifth date, or fiftieth date. You can still get these diseases or get infected. It does not matter how quickly you have sex or how long you wait to have sex. You cannot tell if a person is a carrier just by looking at them or dating them for a short or long period of time.

LAST BUT NOT LEAST: BOUNDARIES. SET AND RESPECT THEM!

People, before you start any dating or relationship, you must set boundaries. You must respect the boundaries set by other people. This is very important in moving forward in any relationship. You must learn when to back off, back up, and back down. People can get too aggressive during the dating process. Slow down; give it time. If it is for you, it is for you. Please watch what you say, do, how you treat a person, and how you allow a person to treat you. I always try to treat a person the way I want to be treated and it has always worked for me.

MY THOUGHTS ABOUT DATING

I was a player for over thirty years. All my relationships were measured in hours, not months or years. Now that I am done with that life, I am trying to find that special lady to have in my life for the rest of my life. I am finding it very difficult to find a lady that knows what she is looking for in a man or needs from a man. I am not saying that women do not know what they want, but like men, they can be dishonest about what they are looking for. The reason why I was so successful in dating and having sex with hundreds of women was because I was always up front and honest with them about the kind of relationship I wanted to have with them. Not all woman agreed to the relationship I wanted to have with them, but they all respected the fact that I told them and let it be their decision to be with me or not. That is what I am finding so hard about dating.

PLEASE be honest with the person you are dating. Let them know up front what you want from them and what they can expect from you. How many times have you met a person and they told you one thing about themselves, only you find out later that he or she is not that person? How many times has a person said the same thing about you? I leave you with this: mean what you say and say what you mean. The real you will come out one day.

THANK YOU GOD, MY FATHER

I would like to thank God for watching over me when I was out in the world doing things I had no business doing. I know if it wasn't for your grace, mercy, favor and blessings, I would have been dead either by someone's hand or HIV or AIDS.

THANK YOU MOM; I LOVE YOU SO MUCH

I'd like to thank the most wonderful mother of all time. Even though you are not with us now, the love I have for you is as strong as the love you had for me. I know I kept you on your knees, praying to God to look over me and keep me safe. I knew the only reason I am still alive is because of your special relationship you had with God. I knew when your prayers reached God's ears, He would listen, look down on you, and say, "No, not Randy again!" Mom, I may not have been the best child you had, but you were the greatest Mother a boy could ask for. Even though you are with God now, I bet you are still worrying God to look after Randy.

THANK YOU, BISHOP AND PASTOR WILLS

I would like to thank my little sister, Pastor Linda Willis, and her husband, Bishop Kevin Willis. They knew my lifestyle and they never judged me. I was always welcome in their home and church.

A VERY SPECIAL THANKS TO PASTOR LINDA WILLIS

I would like to give a very special thanks to my Pastor Linda Willis. Over the years, you have been more to me than a sister. You have been my psychiatrist, spiritual advisor, life coach, and the person I told all of my dark secrets to - and there were a lot. You listened to me and you guided me though all of that madness I had going on in my life - and you never charged me! Thanks. I love you, Little Sister.

THANK YOU, FAMILY

I'd like to thank my family for always telling me, "Boy, you need to get some Jesus in your life." I did and I thank you.

LAST BUT NOT LEAST

To the little, old-school, church-going lady that lived under me in my apartments that would see me bringing all those women up and down the stairs at all times of the day and night: thank you. You never said a word to me. All you did was stand there with her arms folded, shaking your head from side to side, and say to me, "Son, I am praying for you." Thank you and may God bless you all.

BE BLESSED!
YOU CAN FIND ALL MY BOOKS AT
WWW.RANDYBOOKS.NET, AMAZON.COM, AND
BANESANDNOBLE.COM.

www.ingramcontent.com/pod-product-compliance
Lightning Source LLC
Chambersburg PA
CBHW060411290526
45791CB00002B/702